All the Master's Men

*A study of human insufficiency
made sufficient through faith*

ALL THE MASTER'S MEN

KENDRICK STRONG

CHRISTIAN HERALD BOOKS
Chappaqua, New York

Library of Congress Cataloging in Publication Data

Strong, Kendrick

All the Master's Men

Includes index

1. Apostles   I. Title

B52440.S73   225.9'2'2   78-56973

ISBN 0-915684-38-1

FIRST EDITION
CHRISTIAN HERALD BOOKS
40 Overlook Drive, Chappaqua, New York 10514

PERMISSIONS: We acknowledge with appreciation permission to reprint brief passages from

Lord Vanity by Samuel Shellabarger. Little, Brown and Co., 1953.

Erika and the King by Erika Leuchtag. Coward-McCann, 1958.

The Nun's Story by Kathryn Hulme. Little, Brown and Co., 1956.

The Revised Standard Version of the Bible National Council of Churches, 1952.

Documents of the Christian Church by Henry Bettenson. Oxford University Press, 1956, 1963^2.

The Man Who Moved a Mountain by Richard Davis. Fortress Press, 1972.

The Days of Our Years by Pierre Van Paasen. Curtis Brown Ltd., 1939.

PRINTED IN THE UNITED STATES OF AMERICA

In grateful remembrance of
Alexander Converse Purdy
teacher, scholar and friend

TABLE OF CONTENTS

JESUS' DISCIPLES
(using Mark's order for the sequence)

	Matthew 10:2-4	Mark 3:16-19	Luke 6:14-16	John	Acts 1:13
1	Simon Peter	Simon Peter	Simon Peter	Simon Peter	Peter
2	Andrew	Andrew	Andrew	Andrew	Andrew
3	James	James	James	James	James
4	John	John	John	John ?	John
5	Philip	Philip	Philip	Philip	Philip
6	Bartholomew	Bartholomew	Bartholomew	Nathanael	Bartholomew
7	Matthew	Matthew	Matthew		Matthew
8	Thomas	Thomas	Thomas	Thomas	Thomas
9	James	James	James		James
10	Thaddeus	Thaddeus	Judas	Judas	Judas
11	Simon	Simon	Simon		Simon
12	Judas Iscariot	Judas Iscariot	Judas Iscariot	Judas Iscariot	Judas Iscariot
13					Matthias

Preface

JESUS told a story about a man who had come into some money and had decided to build a house. But he let a tricky real-estate agent sell him a lot in an ancient water-course where sand and silt went down twenty feet. During a cloudburst the water raced down the shallow valley, washing the support from under the foundation so that the house was swept away.

Jesus then contrasted this builder with another who had bought a lot on higher ground and had mortared his house to the limestone ledge directly beneath. The same storm which demolished the first house beat against this one also, but could work no damage because its foundation reached down to rock.

One can imagine two of Jesus' lukewarm listeners, Jethro and Joses, conducting a post-mortem on the teaching. "Huh! That man should apply the story to himself! He wants to usher in a new kind of society — a Kingdom of God on earth. Well, by gum! He can't do it by himself. He has to have help, expert help."

"That's right. He may be a genius, like my wife says, but that's not enough."

"Exactly! Now, take a look at that motley group he has chosen as his disciples. Oh, I imagine they're decent people and all that. But do they have what this man Jesus needs? Half of them are ordinary fishermen, I'd say; and the only one with any business sense is Levi, the one who calls himself Matthew since he quit collecting taxes for Antipas. And that Simon the Zealot, there's a real rabble-rouser!"

"The one with the red beard?"

"Yes. It looks to me as though in planning for his new Kingdom Jesus hasn't followed his own advice. He's building his house on sand; and when the cloudburst comes, it will fall as flat as Jericho's walls!"

History, of course, has shown that the forecast of these two hypothetical listeners was wrong. Yet a sober analysis of the Gospels indicates that at that moment they had logic on their side. Jesus had drawn to himself a curious assortment of disciples. The early record of their behavior is starkly uncomplimentary, and the initial image they projected must have been one of fumbling ineptness. But they did not stay this way. No individual could live in close proximity to Jesus for perhaps three years and remain the same. The purpose of this volume is to trace that change.

The record begins with Jesus calling Peter and Andrew, then his cousins James and John (Mk. 1:16-20). He followed with Levi-Matthew (Mk. 2:14). Then for some days there were just these five. It is logical to assume that during this time Jesus observed the behavior of everyone showing interest in him, deciding which of them had the greatest potential. When he was ready, he went up into the hill country and spent the night in prayer. The next morning he chose another seven, apparently from those who had remained with him for the night: Philip and Bartholomew, James the brother of Matthew, Thomas, Thaddeus-Judas the brother of James, Simon the Zealot and Judas Iscariot.

Why did Jesus call them? In the classical tradition, a disciple is one who is received into intimate companionship with a master-teacher. The Twelve whom Jesus selected were to be apprentices in a soul-shaking Kingdom Crusade which would extend "far down the future's broadening way." They were to serve a variety of purposes. Jesus needed them to be his constant comrades, serving his needs; to be in a continuous learning situation with him twenty-four hours a day; to further his Cause by learning how to witness to it; and to carry on that Cause after his death.

These are demands of a high order. Could the Twelve meet them? The most likely reaction to such a question at that time would have been that of our imaginary listeners, Jethro and Joses. The Gospels offer almost no bouquets to the disciples; instead, the records overflow with instances of what Jesus reproachfully termed "failure to understand," "dullness," and "hardness of heart." As a group they are complimented only twice (Mt.19:27,28; Lk.19:39,40).

Does this suggest that Jesus was an unappreciative taskmaster who did not believe in encouragement as an incentive to learn? Not at all. Such behavior would be totally inconsistent with his character as it emerges clearly in the Gospels. It means simply that the disciples, engaged in a severely difficult learning process in which most of their spiritual values had to be turned topsy-turvy, had more failures than successes through most of their months with Jesus. How human they were, and how contemporary with us! In their sandals, and limited to their backgrounds, who today would have done any better?

Although the Bible is rich with many different colors, it contains no whitewash. So to study the disciples — the twelve foundation-stones of the Christian church — is to become acquainted with a dozen men who their Hebrew school classmates might never have characterized as "most likely to succeed." They were lower or middle class laymen, largely ignorant of the cultural ferment of their times. Only Peter, pre-

sumably, was married, and it is likely that none was as old as
Jesus. Numbers of them lacked formal education, and some
may have been illiterate. Few had been a hundred miles from
home. All but Judas had been raised in the unsophisticated
uplands of Galilee. Their insight may have been blurred by
the spiritual astigmatism of the day. Every belief was neatly
pigeon-holed in separate categories and tightly sealed against
the admission of light. No wonder some of the better-edu-
cated observers dismissed with a shrug the Kingdom Cause.
Its personnel, they felt, had feet of clay.

And yet the dire predictions never came true. The Kingdom Crusade survived its leader's death. The burden of pilot-
ing the Cause came to rest on the shoulders which few had
thought would be strong enough to receive it. To everyone's
astonishment, presumably including that of the disciples
themselves, the foundations were not shaken and the house
did not fall. There are today eight hundred million Christians
as proof—men, women and children who should be regarding the Twelve in warmest appreciation. It is fascinating
to see how this growth came about, and there is wisdom in
the Bible's revelations for us today. In a sense, the story is a
study of human insufficiency made sufficient by faith.

The "RSV" in the Scripture references indicates that the
translation employed is that of the Revised Standard Version,
copyrighted by the Christian Education Division of the National Council of Churches, and used by permission. All other
references are from "The Gospel Digest: A Vernacular Version,"
which is my own unpublished rendition.

This survey of the human material which Jesus used begins by trying to find answers from the biblical record to three
questions: 1) What were the disciples like? 2) How did Jesus
try to change them? 3) What was the result? Then follows a
personal portrait of each disciple, insofar as the record makes
such data available.

Chapter One

The Twelve

I. What Were They Like?

THE only accurate way to find out what Jesus' disciples were like is to examine every bit of information about them in the Gospels and Acts in the light of the question: "Just what is going on here?" As has been intimated, the answers are somewhat disconcerting, being rarely complimentary to the Twelve. They reveal that the "dowry" which they brought to Jesus' Kingdom Crusade consisted mainly of attributes which the Master would have to reshape or develop if the disciples were to become the foundation-stones of that Kingdom. The record indicates five basic characteristics, each negative, but paired with a positive potential. The disciples were:

- Closed-minded, but with a readiness to be teachable;
- Self-centered, but able to become obedient;
- Self-distrustful, but willing to grow in self-confidence;
- Fearful, but able to emerge into trust;
- Skeptical, but ready to move into faith.

Let us consider several typical illustrations of each characteristic.

A. Closed-mindedness

1. The Parable of the Soils reveals how closed the minds of Jesus' disciples were. "Jesus began to teach by the lakeshore. Because a great number of people gathered to hear him, crowding right down to the beach, he was forced to get into a boat and sit in it a few feet from shore. From there he taught spiritual truths by means of parables such as this one:

"'Listen! A farmer once went out to seed his fields. As he sowed, some of the seed dropped along the footpath where the birds quickly found and ate it. Some of the seed fell on rocky stretches with little topsoil where it sprouted quickly; but unable to put down roots, the seedlings were soon wilted by the noontide heat of the sun. Some of the seed fell among weeds which shot up more quickly and choked the life from the grain before it headed out. But some of the seed fell on rich soil where it grew to maturity, bringing at harvesttime a yield of thirty or sixty or possibly a hundred times the amount of seed sown.'

"Jesus concluded by saying, 'If you are attentive, you will pay heed'" (Mk.4:1-9).

But the parable left the disciples confused rather than enlightened. A parable has been defined as an earthly story with a heavenly meaning. They understood the earthly meaning, but its spiritual application eluded them. So later on they ask Jesus to explain. He may well have regarded this parable as among his most inspired, and he may have been keenly disappointed with the obtuseness of his followers. Something of that disappointment shows in his reply:

"Do you actually not understand this parable? How then will you understand any of the others?" (Mk.4:13).

Having rebuked them, he then gave them the interpretation: "The man who sows is the one who spreads the Good News. The seed scattered along the path symbolizes the man who hears the message of the Kingdom and does not welcome it; then the Evil One appears and steals what is sown in his heart. The seed dropped onto rocky soil symbolizes the person who joyfully accepts the message but does not give it total allegiance. Although it may survive briefly in his life, the moment it causes him trouble or persecution he lapses into his former unbelief. The seed which fell among weeds symbolizes the one who receives the message but who permits worldly concerns and the tenacious pursuit of wealth to crowd out its influence. The seed which fell on good soil symbolizes the man who both hears and heeds the message. Coming to full harvest in his life, the Good News multiplies itself thirty times, sixty times, or even one hundred times" (Mk.4:14-20).

As the disciples absorbed this interpretation, they grew a bit in understanding.

2. But not enough. For shortly thereafter, Jesus gave the Parable of the Weeds: " 'You enter the Kingdom of Heaven in this manner. A man once sowed good seed in his field, but in the dead of night his enemy came, sowed weeds among the wheat, and stole away undetected. When the crop sprouted and grew toward maturity the weeds grew also. Then the hired men came to the farmer and asked, "Didn't you sow clean seed? Why are there so many weeds?"

" 'The farmer replied, "My enemy must have done this!"

" ' "What do you want us to do?" they asked. "Try to weed the fields?"

" ' "No," he replied, "because you would pull up too much wheat. Instead, let everything grow together till harvest, when I will tell the reapers to gather the weeds into bundles first and burn them, and then to bring the wheat into my granary" ' " (Mt.13:24-30).

"As soon as the crowd had dispersed the disciples clustered around Jesus and said, 'Please explain to us the parable of the weedy field.' With an inward sigh Jesus complied. 'The farmer who sowed the good seed is the Son of Man; the field is the world; the good seed represents those who will inherit the Kingdom; the weeds are the sons of the Evil One; the enemy who sowed them is the devil; the harvest is the end of the world; the reapers are angels.'

" 'Just as a reaper collects the weeds and tosses them onto a bonfire, so also at the end of the world the Son of Man will send out his angels to sort out from his Kingdom everything which is wicked and everyone who is evil, and to cast them out—in spite of their protestations and tears—into the roaring furnace. But the righteous who remain in the Kingdom of their Father will shine as brightly as the sun. You who are listening, heed these words' " (Mt.13:37-43).

The complexity of this parable makes it almost an allegory—in which every detail serves an appointed task—so our sympathy may go out to the disciples. Which of Jesus' modern followers would have done any better? We understand it today because we have known the explanation as long as we have known the parable. But by their questions the disciples continued to learn.

3. Mark, who received much of his material straight from Peter, reports that one day Jesus taught a large crowd well past the noonhour, and the disciples began to get hungry. Finally they whispered to Jesus, "Why don't you knock it off for a while, so that these people can go and find some lunch?"

Jesus replied, "Why don't you give them something to eat?"

The disciples were flabbergasted and replied in effect, "Are you kidding? There must be five thousand people here. Where are we to get fifty dollars for food?" (Mk.6:35-37).

Caught in the extreme literalism for contemporary Jewish thought, which provided little room for either imagination or humor, they failed to understand that Jesus' words were not idle talk, and that Jesus was talking about something more than just food. He was preparing them for an experience of table fellowship foreshadowing the Last Supper—the feeding of the multitudes.

After the crowd had been fed, Jesus issued to the disciples his strongest-yet rebuke. "Why are you still complaining about having no bread? Don't you understand yet? Are you purposefully being stupid? Having eyes, are you blind, and having ears, are you deaf?" (Mk.8:17,18). He then reviewed briefly the feeding of the thousands, and asked, "Surely you understand now!" (Mk.8:21). But no answer followed.

4. John relates that when the disciples returned with groceries to the well near Sychar and had recovered from their astonishment at finding Jesus in conversation with a Samaritan — and a woman at that! — they prepared lunch and urged him to eat.

Jesus had just been speaking with the woman about his messianic mission. He knew that his fundamental support for this mission came not from any earthly source such as bread and cheese, dates and wine, but from God. Grateful that his relation to his Father was indeed providing that strength, and that his disciples had not yet learned how to appropriate it for themselves, he replied, "I have food to eat that you do not know about." By this time the disciples should have learned to examine any cryptic statement of Jesus for its inner meaning, but as usual they took him literally. They began whispering among themselves, "Has someone brought him food? That woman?" But Jesus, knowing that they had failed to understand again, said, "My food is to do God's will and finish his work" (Jn.4:27-34).

5. Again, the Pharisees had complained to Jesus that he and his disciples did not follow the ancient tradition of ceremonially washing the hands before eating. Jesus promptly discomfited them by showing how they consistently violated the Commandment, "Honor your father and mother." He concluded with a scathing denunciation of their lip-service to God and then, to the crowd which had gathered, he added, "It isn't what goes into a man's mouth which defiles him, but what comes out of it" (Mt.15:1-11).

This time Peter, on behalf of the other disciples, asked

Jesus to explain. Still on edge from his encounter with the hostile Pharisees, Jesus replied, "Are you as stupid as all the rest? Whatever is eaten goes into the digestive tract and so out of the body. But what comes out of the mouth comes from the heart. What truly defiles an individual, then, are words indicative of wicked thoughts — murder and adultery, sexual perversion and theft, perjury and slander" (Mt.15:15-19). This is quite obvious when one thinks about it, but the disciples had been unwilling to think.

6. The same obtuseness was shown in response to Jesus' teaching about the permanence of family relationships. "When he was asked, 'May a man lawfully divorce his wife?' Jesus asked in reply, 'What was Moses' teaching?'

" 'Moses permitted a man to divorce a woman simply with a written statement,' came the reply.

"Jesus said, 'He allowed this procedure only because you will not understand and follow God's law. For back at the beginning, during the creation, God made human beings both male and female. Therefore a man shall cease giving primary allegiance to his parents and give it to his wife, so that in the act of union the two shall become one flesh. Instead of being two separate people, then, they have become one. When God thus joins a couple, no man may separate them' " (Mk.10:2-9).

This teaching seems clear enough to us today, even though the divorce rate denies it. Many forms of the marriage service still conclude the words of union with the King James translation of verse 9: "Whom God hath joined together, let no man put asunder" — especially a judge! Marriage is to be a life-long contract. Yet as soon as the disciples were within the privacy of a house, they asked Jesus to explain further. Was this another teaching too radical for them because it was at variance with Moses' Law, with which their minds were saturated? We are not told.

7. Mark also relates that Jesus had once warned his disci-

ples that his role as earthly leader of the Kingdom Crusade would be ended by his execution. They refused to take the prophecy seriously. When he warned them a second time, the record states simply, "They did not understand what he meant, and were afraid to ask him" (Mk.9:32). They who for months had pestered him for further explanations of many teachings, now suddenly clammed up. Having finally been persuaded of Jesus' personal danger and his acceptance of it, did the disciples see something of the Master's inflexible decision in his face which discouraged argument? Or was their reaction possibly an expression of the "turtle syndrome" — if they ignored such bad news and withdrew into their shells, the danger might go away? Whatever the reason — and it is not made plain — here again was a grievous failure to understand.

8. Then came the "Triumphal Entry," one of the most misnamed events in history. Before Jesus dramatically entered Jerusalem, he had doubtless explained to his disciples what his intentions were. Both Matthew's and John's accounts include the key verse from Zechariah which Jesus must have quoted to them:

> Rejoice greatly, O daughter of Zion,
>   Shout aloud, O daughter of Jerusalem!
> Lo, your king comes to you;
>   triumphant and victorious is he,
> humble and riding on an ass,
>   on a colt, the foal of an ass (9:9 RSV).

Jesus was indicating to them, as he would to the crowds along the branch-strewn road, that he was not a heroic military liberator or political superman, but a suffering Messiah of humble servitude.

Yet when they reached Jerusalem, John's account bluntly indicates that the disciples had missed the point of this most vital of Jesus' teachings. "The disciples did not understand then what he was doing. But after he had gone to glory, they remembered both that this had been written about him and that he had experienced it" (Jn.12:16). Mental rigidity prevented them from accepting anything but the prevailing concept of messiahship then in vogue—which Jesus could not accept for himself. Here again was failure to understand, right at the beginning of Passion Week!

But here also is a preview that things will get better. Under successive hammerblows—the arrest, the crucifixion and the resurrection—the veil that covered their minds which Jesus had striven so continuously to remove was torn away. The full knowledge of what the Kingdom Crusade meant and would cost at last became clear to them. Then their full powers were released for the tasks Jesus had entrusted to them.

Three observations from these eight incidents indicate the potential for growth which Jesus had seen in the disciples.

A. Slow to understand though they were, the disciples were rarely afraid of asking questions. They were at ease with Jesus, and did not often dissemble their feelings for fear of rejection or ridicule. They were not afraid of admitting their ignorance. That they wanted to learn is evident in the above instances—a fact of which Jesus made full use.

The headmaster of a renowned Scottish academy, when facing an applicant for admission, would say, "Now listen closely." He would then deliver a three-minute lecture on Neo-Platonism in St. John's Gospel. When finished, he would fix the applicant with a basilisk eye and say, "Now, young sir, did you ken what I was saying?" If, in an ill-judged attempt to act more intelligent than he was, the applicant would reply smartly, "Yes, sir!" the headmaster would snort, "Then you are wiser than I am, for I really did not ken much of it myself! You may go." And across the application he would write, "Unteachable. No hope!"

But when an applicant with greater intellectual honesty if

not ability replied falteringly, "I'm afraid I didn't understand, sir." the headmaster would beam, shake his hand and say, "You may report at the beginning of the next term." On the application he would write, "Teachable. Hope!"

The questions the disciples asked did not indicate stupidity. They were caused by the mental rigidity toward all things religious which characterized Judaism at that time. Jesus' battles with his disciples for full understanding was a microcosmic section of his battle with all mankind, both then and now. He was dealing with a stratum of religious thought far above that in which people ordinarily moved. The disciples may have been slow of heart, but they recognized it and were willing to grow out of it. They had the saving grace of teachableness.

B. It is interesting to note also that they were sensitive about their closed-mindedness. They never let on that they hadn't understood till the crowds were gone and they were alone with Jesus. They were embarrassed by their failures, and wanted no one but Jesus to know. Who today would not have felt the same way? It was in the private conversations which followed their questions, that they gained new insights which they would otherwise not have received. And we, too, have benefitted, for frequently Jesus carried his discourses further with them than he did in public. If the disciples had not requested explanations, very likely the Gospel records would have been the poorer—and so would we.

C. However unhappy Jesus was with their obtuseness— and there is plenty of evidence that he was—he never let his impatience distract him from giving full answers to their questions. A lesser teacher might have exclaimed irascibly, "You heard me once. How many more repetitions do you need? How do I know if you'll get it even if I go over it twenty times?" But because Jesus knew that his disciples were teachable, he put aside any possible irritability at their insensitivity and took time to explain things carefully. Why?

An old wood-carver in Brienz was asked by a teenager

why he worked so patiently at details as he carved a mountain goat. The craftsman replied, "This carving will be around long after I am dead. Because I will no longer be able to uphold the guild standards of excellence, I hope that other craftsmen, as they come after me, will see in my carvings the embodiment, the incarnation, of those standards."

Similarly, the disciples were being shaped by Jesus for the task of continuing his Kingdom Crusade after his death. Master craftsman that he was, Jesus spent the requisite amount of time on details, so that the men he was shaping would bear faithful witness of his fresh standards of excellence down through the long years. And we today are witnesses to the lofty quality of his teaching ability.

B. Self-centeredness

In addition to being closed-minded, the disciples entered the Kingdom Crusade with the additional handicap of being self-centered. This, of course, is where almost everyone enters. In its normal state, humankind is continually placing itself at the center of the universe. Because we are "of the earth, earthy," made of dust, we are by nature arrogantly centered about our own dusty experiences. We have the "me-first complex":

> Who helps the "greatest number" upon earth
>   Shall know the "greatest good" is always done:
> For of all numbers, which has greatest worth?
>   It is that sovereign digit, "Number One!"

For a long period the disciples were no different. The way God wanted them to live, as explained and exemplified by Jesus, held little compulsion for them. It interfered drastically with their desired lifestyle. It conflicted with their "I want" instincts. Even after being with Jesus month after month, watching his example of Kingdom behavior, listening to him tell how to follow it themselves, they must have decided,

"Well, he can go on that way if he wants, but it's not for me!"
Thus in every age and clime some Christians have refused to
"give heart and soul and mind and strength to serve the King
of Kings." They have sat on the outskirts of the Crusade rather
than where the action has been. The disciples too were slow
in learning that one's greatest freedom to be himself comes
only through the Christlike discipline described by George
Matheson:

> Make me a captive, Lord,
>   And then I shall be free;
> Force me to render up my sword,
>   And I shall conqueror be.

This is but a rhymed and metered rendition of Paul's words to
the lay-people in Corinth: "For he who was called in the Lord
as a slave is a freedman of the Lord. Likewise he who was free
when called is a slave of Christ" (I Cor.7:22 RSV). But the disciples
did not accept this truth. Rather, they were the epitome of
self-centeredness. Jesus was discouraged with them many
times. With clarity the Scriptural record reveals the ways in
which their selfishness appeared in self-preservation, self-
preoccupation and self-conceit.

1. Self-preservation

A. Mark relates an incident early in Jesus' ministry in
which the disciples thought their lives were in danger. "That
evening Jesus said to his disciples, 'Let us cross over to the
other side of the lake.' After telling the crowd to go home they
set out in the boat from which he had been preaching, with
other small boats accompanying them. A heavy storm arose,
washing great waves over the gunwales and nearly swamping
the boat. Jesus was at the stern, asleep on a cushion.

"The disciples shook him awake, crying, 'Master, don't you
care if we all drown?'

"Jesus stood and, rebuking the elements, exclaimed, 'Qui-

et down! Be still!' The wind died away till not a breath of air
stirred. Then Jesus said to them, 'What has become of your
faith, that you should be so afraid?'

"They were filled with awe and whispered to each other,
'Just who is this man who can control the wind and the
sea?'" (Mk.4:35-41).

The storm, against which they were powerless, had put
the fear of death into them, so that they woke Jesus with
urgent words.

Whenever an individual's life is threatened, adrenalin
pours into his bloodstream. This is one of nature's ways of
supporting him in time of crisis, but it can also have a variety
of side effects. Thus when a child has a narrow escape from
death, one parent may furiously berate the other for careless-
ness, even though the accusation may be totally undeserved.

A deacon of a church I served during World War II suddenly stopped attending when his son was drafted and sent
to New Guinea. I went to his home to inquire about his ab-
sence. He refused to let me in, speaking through the screen-
door. His face was drawn into harsh lines and his voice trembled. His body-language shouted that he was gripped by
fear—fear for the life of his only son.

"You want to know when I'm coming back to church, Reverend?" he asked. "Well, I'll tell you! God has taken my boy
from me, and only when he sends him safely back home
again—and not until then—will I go back to his house." Religion was the innocent victim of his anger, which was a by-
product of his fear for the life of his son.

Now, the disciples' lives—by far their most treasured pos-
session—were threatened by the storm. Because it was useless to rail against the wind and wave, their fear wanted some
other outlet. They lashed out, therefore, against their soundly
sleeping Master for not saving them. Perhaps one reason they
had followed Jesus so faithfully was that they felt secure in
his presence. No harm could come when he was with them.

But now their sense of security was shattered. The storm had drenched such unrealistic optimism. It had not occurred to them before that to follow Jesus might be dangerous. At this point in their experience the disciples were not prepared to make basic personal sacrifices for the Kingdom Crusade.

A young girl I once knew fell victim to a rare disease. She needed a transfusion of blood from another individual who had contracted the same disease and had recovered. The only person who could be found on short notice was the girl's ten-year-old brother. Explaining that it was a life-or-death emergency, the doctor asked the boy if he would give blood to help his sister get well. The lad hesitated a moment and then agreed. While he was on the table, with the blood flowing into a flask, he turned his head toward the doctor and in a small voice asked, "How soon am I going to die?" He had misunderstood the dimension of the donation asked of him; but to his young mind the ultimate was not too much to give for his sister. The attending physician knew, in a compassionate flash of insight, that the boy's initial hesitation had marked a brief battle in which self-preservation had been defeated by self-sacrifice.

Many more months were to pass before the disciples' deliberate choice of self-sacrifice would win as heroic a victory over self-centeredness as did that small blood-donor. And it finally happened only because they had come to discover something of greater value than their own lives.

B. Again at the Last Supper the disciples were told that they had completed their apprenticeship and now were commissioned workers in the Kingdom Cause. "From now on I do not call you servants, because a servant is ignorant of his master's affairs. Rather, I have called you friends, for I have told you everything that I have heard from my Father. You have not chosen me; I have chosen you, and challenge you to live with continuing fruitfulness. When you do this, my Father will give you whatever you ask in my name" (Jn.15:15,16).

Then Jesus led them in his "high-priestly prayer" of conse-
cration, thanking God for them, expressing his trust in them
and committing them into the divine keeping so that his joy
might be fulfilled in them.

The disciples must have been deeply moved by this commissioning service, and yet fear came unbidden into the
Upper Room. Before the evening was over one of the Twelve
sneaked out to guide the authorities to the Garden of Gethsemane — the act of betrayal which led to both Jesus' death
and his own. Nine others would flee in terror to the safety of
the underbrush, and only two — John and Peter — would
show that they were worthy of the faith which Jesus had
expressed in his prayer. And even then the count would drop
to one when Peter's courage finally evaporated in the courtyard of the high priest's palace.

In a short story, "None But the Mighty," Alexander Jensen
depicts a father who has come to the aid of his son, a young
country doctor being sued for malpractice by an influential
family.

The father says, "I concede that you've lined up good legal
talent, but you need more support than that. What about
your friends, the ones you've written to us about — Jack Par-
sons, Orville What's-his-name and the others?"

"I guess they're the victims of social pressure, Dad. They
haven't actually gone over to 'the enemy,' but they have deserted me. I suspect that they are afraid to associate with me,
so they just stay away."

The older man nodded. "And that desertion has the same
effect as betrayal!"

Exactly! Matthew put it succinctly: "Then the disciples
abandoned him and took to their heels" (Mt.26:56). True
enough, it was fear of death and not social pressure which
lent speed to their flight. But in thus deserting him, each one
of the disciples fulfilled Jesus' prophecy that someone that
very night would betray him!

2. Self-Preoccupation

Through Mark's Gospel we see a different facet of the disciples' primary concern for self—how they let petty discomforts irritate them into insensitivity to spiritual truth. "In the crowd was a woman who for twelve years had been troubled by hemorrhages, having been victimized by many doctors who took her money without curing her but only made her worse. Having heard of Jesus, she said to herself, 'If I touch nothing more than his clothes, I shall be made well.'

"Working her way through the crowd till she was directly behind Jesus, she touched his coat. Immediately her hemorrhaging ceased, and she knew she had been healed.

"Sensing intuitively that healing power had flowed out of him, Jesus faced the crowd and asked, 'Who touched my clothes?'" (Mk.5:25-30).

Just what was going on here? Well, Jesus' teaching had been interrupted by Jairus' urgent plea to go to his home and heal his daughter. The day was hot, the road was dusty, perhaps it was past the lunch hour, and people swarmed around Jesus and his companions. Whatever the reason, the disciples were irritated with the situation. Then, in the middle of the pressing crowds, Jesus turned around and asked, "Who touched me?"

To the disciples it may have sounded like the complaint of a child: "Mama, Elizabeth just hit me!"

"Aha!" they may have thought, "Jesus has finally let the heat and the jams of people get to him. Now he knows how we've been feeling for this past hour! He's never complained about crowds before, and now all of a sudden he's demanding to know who shoved him!"

Feeling free, then, to express their own exasperation with the total situation in which they were caught, they replied impatiently, "Look at the crowd around you, Master. Everybody has been jostling us for hours—just everybody. And now you want to put the blame on just one."

Being preoccupied with their own discomforts, they believed that Jesus was relieving his own irritation, just as that
deacon in my church had done, by picking on an innocent
party. Human nature so dictates. They knew *they* acted in this
fashion, so why not he also?

> Though trouble-prone was Si McCann,
>   His days plumb-filled with strife,
> He took his troubles like a man —
>   He blamed them on his wife!

People who are preoccupied with their own concerns assume that other people must be the same.

But the assessment of blame in order to relieve his own
discomfort had been furthest from Jesus' mind. He had felt a
sudden drain of spiritual energy and knew at once that it had
flowed into someone in the crowd. It was important to find
out who it was, because here was a remarkable expression of
faith. A life had been changed while the disciples carped.
Their preoccupation with their own petty irritations had re-
duced their spiritual sensitivity to zero.

Some years after World War II, I talked with Kenneth Shad-
ley who, during the saturation bombings of London, served as
a fire-warden in the area about St. Paul's Cathedral. He told
me that a bomb had caught the early evening traffic and
strewed death and destruction over several blocks. A fellow-
warden and he were sorting through victims, seeing who had
the most immediate need for medical attention at the little
first-aid stations that had been hastily erected.

"There were many horrors that night," he recalled, "and
many deeds of quiet heroism. I remember a man with a leg
shattered below the knee. When I knelt beside him, he said,
'Your buddy's put a tourniquet on me. I'm all right for now. I
wish you'd take a look at that gentleman over there.'"

He paused and then added, "And I think that the greatest
horror was a man whose shoes were blown off, running from

station to station, hysterically demanding that the aids bandage his split thumbnail."

By contrast consider this vignette from Italian history. When Giuseppe Garibaldi roused his fellows to strike for a unified nation, he did not promise them comfortable success and bountiful rewards. Rather, he cried, "I am going out from Rome. Let those who wish to continue the war against the stranger come with me. I offer neither pay, nor quarters, nor provisions. I offer hunger, thirst, forced marches, battle and death. Let him who loves his country in his heart, and not with his lips only, follow me." This has the same ring as the words Jesus used with would-be disciples: "Foxes have dens, birds have nests, but the Son of Man is utterly without material security" (Lk.9:58).

Even though relatively tiny, the moon can eclipse the sun. In like manner the disciples often allowed their petty discomforts to loom so large that they blotted out everything more important. In this instance they denied themselves participation in Jesus' dramatic act of healing. Many more months were to pass before the disciples were willing to replace their self-preoccupation with self-forgetfulness.

3. Self-conceit

This unhappy trait showed up in the disciples primarily in two forms. One was a self-assertiveness rooted in their assumption that they were leaders in a new religious Establishment which would replace the present one centered at the Jerusalem temple. The other was a self-importance stemming from their being the closest confidants of the one who headed the Kingdom Crusade under God's mandate.

A. Self-assertiveness. The tendency toward arrogance, induced by the disciples' pride in being charter-members of the Crusade, appeared quite early. "Certain persons had brought little children to Jesus so that he might bless them" (Mk. 10:13). This is not just a New Testament phenomenon. What popular

office-seeker has not had babies lifted up for him to kiss! An
elderly resident of my hometown told me that when he was
five he had been boosted in his father's arms to receive a
blessing from presidential candidate William Jennings Bryan,
his family's hero.

"I was so deeply impressed," he recalled, "that for days I
could almost feel the gentle pressure of his hand on my head.
I refused to wear a cap for fear it would drive the feeling
away."

Similarly, parents whose lives had been deeply marked by
Jesus wanted their children also to be touched by his holy
power. How natural, and how heart-warming!

But then Officiousness Incarnate intervened. The record
continues: "But the disciples rebuffed them" (Mk.10:13). Quite
possibly they had become increasingly sensitive to their Master's needs. It may have been late in the day, when Jesus was
weary of the pressing crowds and their constant hunger for
his teaching. After all, did not the New Order depend entirely
on Jesus, and must not the disciples therefore shield him
even from his well-wishers? Thus their self-assertiveness,
born of their belief that they had a privileged relation to Jesus,
took the form of over-protectiveness. And they were not blind
to the fact that in protecting the Master's interests they were
also defending their own.

So when parents began crowding in, they exclaimed,
"Here, what are you doing? Can't you see that the Master is
worn out? Don't bother him with such foolishness. The Kingdom is not concerned with infants. Go away and let him rest."

Irritation usually raises the voice, so Jesus overheard
them. He was dismayed at the disciples' officiousness on his
behalf. Mark bluntly states, "He was indignant and said to
them, 'Always let little children come to me; never keep them
away, for they, too, have rights in the Kingdom of God. I tell
you earnestly that whoever fails to welcome the Kingdom
with childlike faith will also fail to enter it.' Then gathering the

children in his arms, he laid his hands on them in blessing" (Mk.10:14).

It was only by virtue of lessons such as this that the disciples gradually matured out of self-assertiveness into self-restraint.

B. Self-importance. That Jesus had not yet convinced the disciples of the certainty of his martyrdom is indicated in the ninth chapter of Mark. "They went through Galilee as secretly as possible because Jesus was teaching his disciples and saying, 'The Son of Man will be betrayed into the hands of his enemies, and they will kill him; but three days after his death he will rise again.' But they did not understand what he meant, and were afraid to ask him about it.

"When they had come to Capernaum and entered a house, Jesus said to his disciples, 'What were you arguing about along the way?'

"They would not reply, because they had been discussing which of them was the most important of all" (Mk.9:30-34). Who is to be second in command of the new Establishment? Who is to be Dean of the Disciples' Corps, with all its special privileges and honors?

Here was a virulent stage of the dread disease of self-centeredness, stemming from the virus which produces the world's "I-trouble." One can almost hear the disciples advancing claim and counterclaim among themselves:

"Who did he call first? Me!"

"I'm a more faithful follower than you!"

"He listens to me oftener than to you!"

"Whose family is our heaviest contributor?"

"He trusts me more. That's why he gave me the money-bag!"

How reminiscent this is of the couplet chanted by the wicked stepmother in "Snow White":

"Mirror, mirror on the wall,
Who is the fairest one of all?"

Already burdened by foreknowledge of the future, Jesus' spirits must have drooped at this new evidence that self-importance, not the Kindom Crusade, was foremost in his followers' minds. That Crusade was drawing toward a final crisis, and yet their first concern was about rank. Had they learned nothing about the nature of the Kindgom? With an inward sigh Jesus realized that he must fix in their minds a criterion of behavior different from any they were using, different from wealth, position, intelligence, education and the like.

"So gathering the Twelve, Jesus sat down and said to them, 'Whoever wants to be first must choose, instead, to be the least, and become a servant to all'" (Mk.9:35).

Matthew extends the narrative, indicating that Jesus repeated the lesson of several days earlier, which apparently had not been learned. "Calling to him a child, he placed him in their midst. 'Truly I tell you,' he said, 'that unless you do a complete about-face and become childlike, you will never enter the Kingdom of Heaven. Whoever becomes as humble as this little child will be the greatest in the Kingdom of Heaven'" (Mt.18:2-4).

Instead of self-importance, the Christian ideal is self-abnegation. The disciples in their hunger for rank and their need to scratch the itch of their self-conceit were *childish*; the inward attitude which distinguishes the God-inspired disciple is *childlikeness* — a quality highly recommended by Jesus.

Buster Keaton, the sad-faced comedian, frequently found on his doorstep a group of children who had come over to ask it he could come out to play! If he had gone to their houses with a parallel request, or if he had sourly rejected their innocent invitations, it would have been childish on his part. But in spontaneously accepting their overtures and joining in their games, he revealed a childlikeness which his family and friends came to treasure. The two qualities, as the disciples gradually discovered, are poles apart.

As one reviews the biblical record of the disciples' thoughts and actions, so often motivated by selfishness, one is amazed that the Kingdom Crusade ever survived Jesus' death. How much of his effort had to be directed toward transmuting their instincts of self-preservation, self-preoccupation and self-conceit into the opposite trait of self-surrender! But his efforts paid off, for after the disciples had passed through the crisis of their own betrayals of him, they emerged into persons whose quality of self-surrender the present-day followers of Jesus would do well to copy!

C. Self-distrust

It may seem curious that the disciples, marked as they were by excessive self-centeredness, should also have been characterized by self-distrust. How odd that they who had bickered over rank in the Kingdom should also show evidences of an inferiority complex! Yet the two qualities are not mutually exclusive. Self-distrust is possible to those who are self-centered, and sense within themselves flaws which normally might not show. Self-distrust is the uneasy realization that we are actually not as good as the image of ourselves we cherish and like to hold up on display. It can be a wholesome sign, an indication that our self-image is unrealistic.

The self-centered person believes he can do everything through his own strength and skill. Yet in a time of severe testing he usually learns that his own resources and abilities are not sufficient, and he cries in effect, "Lead me to the rock which is higher than I!" (Ps.61:2 RSV). Only after he has begun to move out of self-centeredness into a commitment to the Christian Way does he learn the joy vibrant in Paul's exuberant testimony: "I can meet every situation because Christ gives me the power!" (Phil.4:13).

1. A Humbling Experience

The disciples had just such a humbling experience. Jesus,

Peter, James and John were on the Mount of Transfiguration, and "on rejoining the rest of the disciples, they found themselves surrounded by a huge crowd, deep in argument with some scribes. When the people saw Jesus, they surged forward to meet him in excitement tinged with awe.

"He said to the scribes, 'What are you talking about?'

"A man in the crowd answered, 'Master, I brought my son to you because he is possessed by an evil spirit. Not only does it take away his powers of speech, but it also stiffens him and throws him to the ground where he froths at the mouth and grinds his teeth. I begged your disciples to cast it out, but they couldn't.'

"Jesus replied, 'Such an unbelieving lot of disciples you are! How long must I bear with you? How long must I tolerate you? Bring the boy to me.'

"But when they had brought him forward the evil spirit within him, recognizing Jesus, attacked the boy so that he fell to the ground, twisting convulsively and frothing at the mouth.

"Jesus said to the father, 'How long has he been like this?'

"'Since childhood,' the father replied. 'The evil spirit continually tries to kill him by casting him into the fire and into water. So if you can, have mercy on us, please, and help us.'

"'If I can!' exclaimed Jesus. 'Why, everything is possible to the one who has faith!'

"Instantly the father replied, 'I have faith. But give me more, if what I have is not enough.'

"While the crowd pressed in more closely, Jesus spoke sternly to the evil spirit, saying, 'Deaf and dumb spirit, I order you to come out of this child and never enter him again!'

"With a wild cry and a final convulsion the evil spirit came out, leaving the boy lying in a coma on the ground. At once some of the bystanders said, 'He is dead!' But Jesus took the boy's hand, helped him to his feet," (Mk.9:14-27) and returned him, healed, to his father.

"While the crowd exclaimed over the way in which Jesus could command the power of God," (Lk.9:42,43) "the disciples asked him in an undertone, 'Why couldn't we cast out that evil spirit?'

"'Because of the inconstancy of your faith,' Jesus replied. 'I earnestly tell you if your faith is no bigger than a mustard seed, you can say to this mountain, "Move over there!," and it will obey. You will be able to do the impossible. However, this particular kind of evil spirit can be exorcized only by means of prayer and fasting'" (Mt.17:19-21).

Through this experience the disciples' self-assurance must have been cracked enough to let in a bit of saving self-distrust. Their sudden lack of confidence in their own self-sufficiency proved to be a milestone in their spiritual growth.

2. Hidden Guilt

But they were not always so fortunate. During his final meal with them Jesus said, "'I tell you with absolute certainty that one of you now eating supper with me will betray me.'

"They were upset, and one after another they exclaimed, 'Surely it isn't I, is it?'

"He replied, 'He is one of the Twelve who is eating from the same bowl as I. The Son of Man is headed for the fate decreed in the Scriptures, but woe to the man who betrays him! It would be better for that man if he had never been born'" (Mk.14:18-21).

The disciples' reaction to Jesus' flat statement of coming betrayal was quite different from what might normally be expected. Would it not be logical for them to have cried, "Surely, Lord, it can't be so!" or "Well, you can be sure that it isn't I!" or even fiercely, "Which one of us is it, Lord? We'll take care of him!"

But although disturbed, each asks what at first seems to be a peculiar question: "It surely isn't I, is it?" Every one of them asked it, including Judas who, of course, would ask it to find out whether Jesus actually knew of his intentions. But why the others? Had Jesus touched an exposed nerve of some deeply-hidden guilt within them for having been such poor followers? Had they all been entertaining disloyal thoughts? Did each believe that Jesus had detected within him a latent capability to desert him in the rough times ahead, and was confronting him with it? Or was each disciple wondering whether Jesus had gauged his weakness and was predicting that under coming pressure he would betray his Master? Had Jesus come to know him better than he knew himself, and was warning him of an action he was going to take, even though the thought had not yet crystallized in his own mind? Did each ask because he had come to suspect that he could, under sufficient pressure, act traitorously to save his own skin? Unfortunately we are not told which of these thoughts prompted the disciples' queries. But it is evident that they suspected Judas no more than anyone else.

Yet these questions are not academic to disciples of any culture or century who are face-to-face with trouble. What individual knows for sure what he will do under extreme pressure? He knows how he should act, but in the back of his mind there is a nagging doubt as to whether he will succeed. Peter thought he knew how he would act in crisis, and was wrong. Similarly, many a church trustee or deaconess or other devoted layperson has lied or stolen food to feed a family or to escape persecution or danger. During the past fifty years people without number the world over have, to their dismay, done what they had never dreamed they could do.

Thus, just at a time when Jesus most needed their support, the disciples suddenly were unsure of themselves, suspicious of their own loyalty to him, and upset because he would be betrayed by one of them. Within the next twenty-four hours Jesus would be entrusting to these confused individuals the future of his Kingdom Crusade. And because the disciples did carry on the movement after the crucifixion, their self-distrust may have marked a way station in their gradual growth into self-confidence.

D. Fearful

There are many different brands of fear. There is fear of the supernatural, fear of enemies, fear of the unknown, fear of the future, fear of death. The Gospels indicate that during the course of their apprenticeship the disciples yielded to most of them. On at least nineteen occasions Jesus had to say to them, "Do not be afraid!" We have already considered the fear of death; now let us look at two other fears.

1. Fear of the Supernatural

Mark relates that after feeding five thousand people, Jesus sent the disciples by boat across Lake Galilee to Bethsaida. Because they did not start till after dark and were rowing into a head wind, by dawn they were still a distance from shore. Then one of them saw Jesus coming toward the boat, walking on the water. The disciple cried out fearfully, "Look, a ghost!" All of them were terrified. Jesus called, "Stop worrying! It is I. Don't get panicky." When he came into the boat with them the storm died away. Then the fear which they had had of a ghost was changed into fear of Jesus' superhuman powers. The King James Version declares that they were "sore amazed"—badly frightened (Mk.6:47-52). Matthew adds that trembling they knelt, exclaiming, "You are indeed the Son of God!" Doubtless none of them dared to get too close to him till they were safely ashore in broad daylight and the eerie experience had begun to fade in the busy routine of a new day.

It was entirely normal for the disciples to fear the supernatural. Would any modern disciple have acted any differently under identical circumstances? Though their age was considerably more superstitious than ours; we still carry much too large a burden of superstition despite the influence of a more scientific atmosphere. Perhaps the disciples would have required a supernatural experience to make them accept Jesus as Messiah. Wasn't Jesus continually tempted to do that very thing?

2. Fear of Enemies

More than once the disciples showed fear of the religious Establishment. They had every reason to, of course. Some of Jesus' teachings were downright harsh, particularly when directed at his Establishment enemies, the scribes, the Pharisees and the priests. He was continually creating the danger of reprisals. Here are examples:

"You pious frauds! You are so intent on worshiping traditions that you ignore God's commands. You manipulate tradition so as to avoid doing God's will" (Mk.7:6,8,9).

"You are unteachable!" (Mk.10:5).

"It is easier for a camel to wriggle through the eye of a needle than for a rich man to enter the Kingdom of God" (Mk.10:25).

"Beware of the scribes, because they pray long prayers at the same time they are defrauding widows" (Mk.12:40).

'You hypocrites!" (Mt.22:18).

"For them, every deed is a show-off" (Mt.23:5).

"You slam heaven's door in men's faces" (Mt.23:13).

"Blind guides . . . blind fools" (Mt.23:16,17).

"You strain out a gnat and swallow a camel" (Mt.24:24).

"You are like whitewashed tombs, outwardly beautiful, but on the inside filled with corpses and corruption" (Mt.23:27).

There is no doubt but that Jesus was single-handedly taking on the whole religious hierarchy that was holding the Jewish people in spiritual subjugation to a once-essential but now-outmoded Law. He was throwing jagged rocks at the men who guided and sustained that hierarchy. So understandably the disciples began to get nervous. They could see no good in such forthright attacks, and were afraid of a back-lash. Lethal power could be hurled against them in return. The Establishment's "sticks and stones" could indeed "break their bones!" Here was fear of men in high places. There are times when fear is indeed an eminently sensible reaction, and this was one. The trick is not to let it determine conduct.

The disciples finally became so uneasy they approached Jesus on the matter. "Master," they began, "the Pharisees are really angry at what you have been saying. After all, you have been insulting them day after day. Don't you think that you had better be a little more careful in what you say? Direct confrontation with the top authorities is dangerous, Master, and you should avoid anything controversial — at least till the present furor dies down" (Mt.15:12).

Don't tip over any apple carts! Don't poke sticks into wasps' nests! Don't kick sleeping police dogs, especially religious ones!

How often the voice of prudence triumphs over the voice of faith! A major obstacle to any crusader, in addition to an Establishment, is the well-meaning friend who insists that his leader should soft-pedal his beliefs whenever they come into direct conflict with the power structure.

I recall being pulled into an alcove during a reception welcoming my wife and me to a new church. An elderly gentledame wanted to talk with me in private. "Mr. Strong," she began, "as you begin work here I have one bit of advice for your own good, and I trust you will heed it. Never speak against liquor here. This is the one thing the members will not tolerate. A word to the wise is sufficient." As events turned out, she was wrong. Her advice, given with the kindest of intentions, was pernicious.

The temptation to compromise one's convictions comes in all sizes. I once heard Martin Niemoeller in West Berlin describe his life during the war years. Because of his strong anti-Nazi stand many like-minded church people rallied around and ultimately established a "Confessing Synod" with its "Barmen Confession." Shortly thereafter it became evident that some members were offering only lukewarm support. "A good thing can be pushed too far, Martin," they said. "We are commanded in the Scriptures to obey the state, and you are leading us into outright disobedience. Tone down your accusations and oppositions or we will no longer support you. Continue on in your present course, and you will wind up as a guest of the state in some concentration camp!"

With a smile Niemoeller continued, "Well, they were right. When we stepped up our opposition to all that National Socialism was doing, they pulled out and became 'German Christians'—religious Quislings. And I was taken off to concentration camp.

"After a while Hitler sent word to me that if I would promise to stop attacking him, he would let me return to my church. But I replied, 'I hold my commission to preach from God, and he has not revoked it.'

"Hitler's emissary snapped, 'How long, then, do you expect to stay in this place?'

"'Till Hitler and his government are destroyed.'

"The emissary glared at me. 'Then you will stay here till you die,' he shouted, and stamped off.

"To his retreating back I said, 'That, too, is in the hands of God.'"

Niemoeller remained in the camp till the Third Reich went down in flames, a period of more than eight years. He was luckier than Micaiah, an Old Testament prophet who was probably never released from his dungeon; and more fortunate than a fellow pastor, Dietrich Bonhoeffer, who ended on a scaffold.

But Jesus, like Niemoeller, was not about to accept defeatist advice. The religious Establishment was the great stumbling block to the success of the Kingdom Crusade, and must not be bowed to, but overcome. How well Paul perceived this later on and turned his heavy guns on the foundation supporting that Establishment — the Law of Moses! He wrote, "You are cut off from Christ when you try to be made righteous by obedience to the Law. For it is by our faith that the Spirit can give us the righteousness for which we hope" (Gal.5:4,5).

Jesus knew that no soft-pedaling of this truth was possible. So he replied crisply to the disciples' complaint, "There are many weeds in my Father's earthly garden which I must pull up. Those Pharisees are blind guides. You know what happens when a blind man leads a blind man. Both will end up in a ditch!" (Mt.15:13,14).

In speaking in this way Jesus was not underrating the enemy. His shrewd assessment of the situation included the awareness that death was near. But neither prudence nor fear controlled Jesus' life. This is a crucial part of the example he set for his disciples, both then and in every generation to follow.

E. Skeptical

One other area of potential growth remains to be identified: the disciples' skepticism, which would eventually yield to faith. The largest number of examples in the Gospels of this skepticism occur in the days following the crucifixion.

1. Luke reports that when the angel told the two Marys, Joanna and the other woman that Jesus was risen, they ran all the way back to the disciples and poured out their good news. But how were they received? The record states baldly, "Yet what they claimed sounded so improbable that no one believed them" (Lk.24:11). Peter, however, may have been an exception. On the outside chance that the women might be right, "he slipped out and ran to the tomb. Bending down, he saw only the linen sheets inside. Greatly puzzled at what had

happened, he went home again" (Lk.24:12). Perplexed he was, but not persuaded. Perhaps trust flared briefly but it soon sputtered out.

2. Similarly, Matthew reports that an angel said to the two Marys, "Do not be afraid. I know that you are looking for Jesus who was crucified. He is not here, for just as he prophesied he has risen. Come and see the place where he was laid. Then go quickly and tell his disciples he has risen from the dead, and gone ahead of you into Galilee, where you will see him. This is my message to you."

"With awe mingled with overwhelming joy the women immediately left the tomb and ran to tell the disciples the good news. All at once Jesus was there in front of them, greeting them. Running up, they fell down in worship before him, clasping his feet.

"'Don't be afraid,' he said. 'Go and tell my brothers they are to return to Galilee where they will see me'" (Mt.25:5-10).

The disciples trudged northward, perhaps with misgivings, perhaps to Mount Hermon where some believe Jesus was transfigured. There the Master met them. What was their reaction? "When they saw him, most of them knelt in reverence, but some still did not believe" (Mt.28:17). Seeing was not believing!

In Samuel Shellabarger's novel, *Lord Vanity*, a spurious count tells the hero, "My dear boy, if you will only concentrate on one thought, one thought alone, until you have mastered it, you'll be in a fair way of making the world your oyster. And that's the ruling purpose of every intelligent man."

"What thought, your excellency?"

"Simply this. To consider anything or any person a humbug until they prove otherwise."

Here is the quintessence of the skeptical mind! It is perilously close to the skepticism which the disciples showed. To them, the resurrection was still humbug!

In one of the endings of Mark there is a final instance of

the disciples' skepticism. "Later on Jesus appeared to the Eleven as they were eating together. He reproved them for their stubborn unwillingness to believe, particularly since they had doubted eyewitness testimony that he was risen" (Mk.16:14). How could such skepticism have survived for so long in any disciple's heart? It must be one of the hardest traits to dislodge!

II. How Jesus Sought to Change Them

We have examined the raw materials from which Jesus had to shape the future leadership of his Kingdom Crusade. The men he had chosen were closed-minded, self-centered, self-distrustful, fearful and skeptical. They were normal human beings Jesus had to turn into extraordinary ones. By no means hopeless cases, they revealed the potential to become quite different. Skilled teacher that he was, Jesus knew how to nurture the disciples in such a way as to bring their latent capabilities into full bloom. That he succeeded is a fact of history.

How, then, did he guide them so that they grew out of their weaknesses and provided the Apostolic Church with vigorous leadership marked by broad-mindedness, self-surrender, self-confidence, trust and faith? The answer is suggested in Galatians 5:17: "If you are guided by the Spirit you will not fulfill the desires of your lower nature."

In the early years of flight a pilot unexpectedly found one of his controls vibrating oddly. Having driven several rats from the tail of his plane before he left the hanger, he suspected that another rat was chewing at the control cord running from the tail assembly to the cockpit. If the rat chewed through the cord he would crash. Yet there was no way he could frighten off the rat. The airport was twenty minutes away, and the cord would be bitten through before he could reach the ground.

Suddenly he knew what to do. He put his plane into the

steepest climb possible and went from three thousand feet to the highest altitude the craft would go. But although the motor sputtered a bit and he felt slightly giddy because of the thinness of the air, the chewing vibrations gradually ceased. Three minutes later he descended to his normal altitude and continued to the airport. There in the tail section he found not one rat but three, all asphyxiated by the lack of oxygen, and the control cord nearly severed in two places.

Isn't this a parable of how an individual grows spiritually? He learns to live at such a lofty altitude that former habits and temptations simply can't "breathe," and cease to control him. He puts himself so wholeheartedly into what is good that he has neither interest in nor energy for what is bad or even second-rate. He commits himself so fully to the High Way that paths leading downward are ignored. "If you are guided by the Spirit, you will not fulfill the desires of your lower nature."

Jesus knew the power of this truth. So he sought to build within the disciples' hearts such a hunger for the Kingdom of God that no competing self-concern could survive. Tradition-mindedness would atrophy with disuse and open-mindedness would take its place. Deprived of life-giving oxygen by selflessness, self-centeredness would perish. Self-distrust would yield to self-confidence, fear to trust, and skepticism to faith. How could Jesus coax his disciples up to such a vermin-exterminating altitude of the Spirit? Like a good teacher, he had numerous techniques in his kit.

A. Initial Fieldwork

On finishing my freshman year at Beloit College I was sent at the tender age of nineteen to North Dakota as a "ninety-day wonder" to serve as the summer minister of little churches in Granville and Deering. In high school I had felt a call to the ministry and I wanted to gain an on-the-field perspective of the profession for which I would be studying for at least six more years. Although such "externships" are a common practice in home missionary areas and in the study of law, pre-medical students are never given parallel charge of a medical clinic! Such action would send shivers of apprehension and outrage up and down every physician's spine! But the religious Establishment did not have the personnel in those days to protect souls the way the medical Establishment protects bodies. For in those wheat-growing areas I was completely in charge of the spiritual well-being of those two churches. The members accepted me with grace and, hopefully, with patience. All in all, it was an invaluable experience for me, for I was a callow idealist who was familiar only with the church in which I had grown up. It gave me a firsthand view of my future calling.

Matthew relates that early in his ministry Jesus sent his disciples out on a similar test run, or in naval terms, a "shake-down cruise." "Summoning his disciples, Jesus gave them power to cast out evil spirits and to cure even the most severe illness.... He sent them out into the district with these instructions: 'Leave the Gentiles and Samaritans strictly alone, and focus your attention on Israel's religious outcasts. As you go about, preach that the Kingdom of Heaven is already here. Heal the sick, raise the dead, cleanse the lepers, cast out evil spirits. You did not pay for this power, so do not charge for its use. Take no money in your wallet, no knapsack for your back, no extra clothes or shoes or staff. A genuine disciple is worthy of receiving his expenses.' These men were no prodigal sons going forth in luxury to squander their father's resources!

"'And when you come to a town or village, find a reputable citizen to stay with till it is time to leave. When you enter a house, give its members your blessing. If they prove to be deserving of such benediction they will be enriched by it, whereas if they are not worthy to receive it your blessing will return to you untarnished. And when anyone or any village refuses to entertain you or listen to your message, shake its

dust from your shoes as you leave. For I tell you that Sodom
and Gomorrah suffered an easier fate than will that village. So
now I am sending you out like lost sheep among wolves. So
be as wise as snakes but as guileless as doves'" (Mt.10:1,5-16).

Doubtless they went on this first assignment, as I did on
mine, with uneasiness and timidity. But they had it a good
deal rougher than I. Not only were they penniless, with no
monthly check to look forward to, but they were expected to
scrounge for their food, clothing and shelter. And they walked
every mile of their journey, whereas I rode up on to the Great
Plains in a Great Northern railway coach, and found a warm
welcome and provision for every one of my simple needs.

Mark continues the record: "So they went out, preaching
that everyone should repent. They cast out many devils and
healed many sick persons after anointing them with oil"
(Mk.6:12,13). "The apostles then returned and reported to Jesus
everything they had done" (Mk.6:30). By and large, they must
have had an exciting time, and it is a pity that no Gospel
provides details. They had a "preview of coming attractions,"
a glimpse into the larger purposes of the Kingdom and their
share in bringing it to realization among men. Because of this
taste of fieldwork, the daily routine would not seem too bur-
densome and their training so pointless. Everyday chores
would take on significance as necessary details comprising
the larger whole.

B. The Solvent System of Spiritual Strength

After they had made their reports, Mark reports, Jesus
observed that although they were enthusiastic over their experiences they were also drained. They had expended their
normal stamina, both physical and spiritual, and had been
drawing on reserves. On returning, they had walked into a
beehive-like activity. Jesus' place was as busy as any political
headquarters before election day. "Everyone was coming and
going, and no one even had time to eat" (Mk.6:31).

Hubbub was the last thing the disciples needed. Recognizing this and certainly aware of it in himself, Jesus said to them, "Come with me, just by yourselves alone, to some deserted spot where you can relax for a while" (Mk.6:31). He was introducing them to one of his secrets — the solvent system of spiritual strength. A man's soul must follow the same practice as his finances if he is to avoid spiritual insolvency and always have sufficient "capital" for the demands of each day's living. The principle is simply this: withdrawals must be more than equalled by deposits. The consistently overdrawn soul becomes bankrupt. The resources of the Spirit must be renewed with as much faithfulness as they were expended.

Jesus had learned that the water table of his spirit had to be kept high or the water of life would cease to flow. The moment the disciples returned exhausted from their mission was the exact moment for Jesus to show them how he restored his depleted capital so that he remained spiritually solvent: Only by going "far from the madding crowd" and entering into a period of quiet meditation and prayer was he able to sense the presence of God. Only then, freed from distractions and demands, could he open his soul fully to God and through the resulting communion restore the strength he had expended in God's name.

By sharing this secret of strength with the disciples, Jesus provided them a means by which they would gradually grow out of self-centeredness into self-surrender.

C. Instruction in Prayer

On such retreats, which occurred fairly frequently, the disciples learned many things by observing how Jesus spent his time. But when they imitated him by rote, they rarely found the refreshment he did. They sensed that they were just going through exercises without content, which brought a discouragingly small return. So there came a time when a disciple on retreat waited patiently till Jesus had ended his praying, and then asked humbly, "Lord, teach us how to pray, as John the Baptizer taught his disciples" (Lk.11:1).

It would be interesting to know which disciple it was. He should have five stars in his crown! For out of that question came what is now known and loved the world around as the Lord's Prayer. In the 37 words of Luke's version (11:2-4 RSV), and the 31 words in Matthew's (6:9-13 RSV), is found the core of the most heavily used devotional Scripture in all Christendom. More than a prayer, it is the outline of how a prayer should unfold and in what direction it should proceed—a scale-drawing showing the relative importance of petitions, and the mood in which they should be offered. It is a continual witness that prayer at its best is not a self-centered collection of "gimmes" for turning private devotions into personal enrichment. The words "I," "me," or "mine" do not appear. Rather, the prayer is a group-centered instrument for the enrichment of public worship. Furthermore, the words "us" and "our" impart an explicit social dimension. As Walter Rauschenbusch somewhat artily expressed it, "Jesus compels us to clasp hands with our brothers and thus approach the throne together."

This blueprint for the most productive kind of praying was another resource which the disciples used in growing out of self-centeredness and skepticism, into self-surrender and faith. Gradually they came to discover the power inherent in prayer described by Archbishop Trench:

> Lord, what a change within us one short hour
>   Spent in thy presence will avail to make!
>   What heavy burdens from our bosoms take,
> What parched ground refresh as with a shower!
> We kneel, and all around us seems to lower;
>   We rise, and all the distant and the near
>   Stands forth in sunny outline, brave and clear!
> We kneel, how weak! We rise, how full of power!

A new beatitude might well be created, reading: "Happy is the person who knows firsthand the power of prayer."

D. Training in Obedience

The first opportunity Jesus had for giving his disciples an unforgettable lesson in the primacy of obedience to the Kingdom Crusade came early in his ministry. Mark relates that while Jesus was teaching inside a house his mother and brothers appeared. "Standing outside, they sent a message indoors asking him to come out. A crowd was gathered about Jesus when the message came: 'Your mother and brothers are outside, asking for you' " (Mk.3:31,32).

We are never told what his family wanted, which is disappointing because they came almost like a delegation. At one time, you may remember, friends came to take him back home because they thought he was crazy (Mk.3:21). At any rate Jesus showed his innate teaching ability by seizing this small incident in order to drive home to his disciples and others who were listening a supremely important principle of the Kingdom Crusade.

The honoring of one's parents is a command of the Law, and everyone in the group expected Jesus as a dutiful son to break off his teaching and respond to his mother's call. He did, of course, even though Mark did not mention it. But first he had a lesson to teach. For when the message arrived Jesus replied, "Who is truly my mother? Who are truly my brothers?"

"Looking intently at those sitting around him, he said, 'You can be my mother and my brothers; for when you do the will of God you are indeed my brother, my sister or my mother' " (Mk.3:33-35).

In the family of Christ it is not blood but obedience which provides the kindred bond. All are bound to one another and to Jesus by their common devotion to God. The disciples may have needed this reminder, for there is evidence that they frequently assumed they were in God's good graces because they were members of the Kingdom Crusade. Yet actually it was the other way around — they would be authentic members of the Crusade only when they were right with God. Their status did not guarantee the righteousness of their conduct; rather, the quality of their obedience determined their status in the Crusade.

This truth is underscored by the number of children of God-fearing parents who are sentenced to jail each year. A prison chaplain once remarked, "One of my most painful tasks is to help deeply religious parents through their first visit to their child in the penitentiary. They never seem to understand why their boy or girl, raised in what they believe to have been a Christian atmosphere, should have so far departed from the dedication of their childhood. They tell me in sorrowful amazement, 'Why, Charles was baptized!'"

The answer is, of course, that the parents' dedication is never enough. Here is the weakness of infant baptism, unless it is followed later by the recipient's own intelligent confirmation of its meaning in his life. Baptism does not automatically produce faith; it is rather a witness to the faith of the parents. Individuals are members of the Kingdom Crusade not because they are baptized, but because they hunger and thirst for God's righteousness. Obedience, not ecclesiastical status, is the requirement. When Jesus asked James and John, "Are you able?" he meant, "Are you obedient enough?"

Where should obedience be more in evidence than in the church, the Company of the Obedient? Yet many a church is not worthy of this description, in spite of the devoted input of many members. Because of such failure, numerous orders and brotherhoods have appeared, such as the Protestant Community in Taizé near the great Benedictine monastery at Cluny. While there I was given a copy of the "Rule of Taizé," the principles guiding the individual and corporate life of the members. It is a manual of obedience, and without its faithful observance the Community would no doubt deteriorate to a religious social club.

But ought not this intention "to obey God rather than men" also be found beyond the church, in the participation of Christians in the so-called secular pursuits of the home and school, vocation, recreation and politics? Shouldn't families and friends, students and teachers, amphitheater crowds and political parties also be under obedience? How often a marriage fails because only the ties of sex, the presence of offspring or social pressure operate to keep husband and wife together! How often a family splits asunder because vows are forgotten and blood ties are rejected! The validity of the well-known saying, "the family that prays together stays together," is proved by solid statistics; the survival of a marriage or family is most certain when the members are united by a common obedience to God.

In basic military training a soldier is taught obedience in order to create a disciplined body of teamworkers — without which an army would disintegrate into a rabble — to increase his chances of personal survival and to provide an externally directed discipline till his own internally directed self-discipline is produced. In the home, a child is taught obedience for basically the same reasons: to ensure a smoothly running home where the rights of all are protected and the duties of all are fulfilled, to provide for his protection and safety, and to provide that same outside discipline till he can produce his own.

But the Christian is taught obedience for one central reason: complete surrender to the will of God as revealed in the life and death, resurrection and living presence of Jesus. Here is his only authentic certificate of membership in the family of Christ. He may have received numerous church credentials of membership and leadership at local and national levels, but these are only certificates of apprenticeship in the Church Militant. He enters into the select group which com-

prises the Church Obedient only through unqualified surrender of the inner citadel of self to the Almighty.

Thus in all Jesus' instructions to his disciples a dominant
theme is this command of obedience. How much of it did
they understand and accept? Were they pulled toward one
another through obedience to the Lord? Did they gain a
sense of belonging to the family of God through their loyalty
to Jesus? Up to the time of the resurrection the evidence that
this was happening is scanty. Yet the growth must have been
there, occurring deeply within the disciples' souls. Otherwise
there would be no accounting for the sudden flowering of
obedience in their lives at Pentecost, through which the Holy
Spirit could work with compelling power. That obedience
would become so overmastering that it would, according to
tradition, bring all of the disciples but one to martyrdom.

E. The Saintliness of Servanthood

Faced as he was with the everyday evidence the disciples
provided of their preoccupation with self, Jesus continually
taught them the contrasting and liberating saintliness of servanthood. Out of a number of possible examples let us consider two.

1. Matthew tells us Jesus gave his followers a first warning
of his approaching death. "From that day forward Jesus
began to teach his disciples the need to go to Jerusalem.
There he would suffer at the hands of the elders, the Chief
Priests and the scribes, would die, and three days later be
restored to life" (Mt.16:21). At this point Peter took him to task
for such a gloomy prophecy, and was roundly rebuked by
Jesus, who then continued, " 'Whoever would become my
disciple must give up all claim to himself and follow me,
accepting whatever cross may result. For the man who
hoards his life will impoverish it, whereas the man who freely
spends his life on my behalf will enrich it. For what is the
good of gaining the world's wealth by means which shrivel a

man's soul? And what steps could a man ever take to undo such damage? For when the Son of Man appears in the glory of his Father, surrounded by angels, every individual will get exactly what is coming to him' " (Mt.16:24-27).

2. John adds the crowning incident in Jesus' ceaseless efforts to persuade his disciples that servanthood is the ultimate test of devotion to God. He wrote: "Knowing that the Father had given everything into his keeping, and that he had come from God and would return to God, Jesus arose from the supper table. He took off his outer clothes and wrapped a towel around his waist. Then he poured water into a basin and began to wash his disciples' feet, drying them with the towel."

At first Peter refused to receive Jesus' ministrations, but his objections were overcome.

"When he had finished washing their feet and was dressed again, he sat down and said, 'Do you understand what I have been doing? You call me Master and Lord, and this is right, for so I am. And because I, your Lord and Master, was willing to wash your feet, you should be willing to wash one another's feet. I have set an example for you to follow. I tell you earnestly that a servant is not greater than his master, and a messenger is not more important than the man who sends him. You are to be congratulated if, knowing these truths; you actually put them into practice' " (Jn.13:3-5,12-17). Then a few moments later he added, " 'I give you a new commandment — love one another. Just as I have loved you, so you are to love one another. If you can do this, everyone will recognize that you are indeed my disciples' " (Jn.13:34,35).

"I have given you an example!" For centuries groups of Christians have ceremonialized this act of footwashing as an organic part of their observance of the Lord's Supper, and some branches of the Mennonite Church continue this practice today. To act out, literally, this example of Jesus, kneeling in the most humble position one person can assume before another, and then doing the most subservient thing possible — washing and wiping that individual's feet — is so demanding a lesson in servanthood that is usage has almost disappeared.

But not quite. During the June 1972 flood in Rapid City which took 230 lives, survivors were taken to the gymnasium of Central High School for medical care, inoculations, clothing and bedrest. It became evident to the head nurse that a major source of infection could be the bare feet of those who were asleep when the wall of water swept through the city, and whose feet therefore were blackened by mud and slashed by the accompanying debris. A call went out and was answered by students in the Vocational School's Department of Practical Nursing. Armed with the biblical equipment of basin and towel, they went from cot to cot carefully washing the feet and medicating the wounds of several hundred persons.

It is more likely, of course, that our opportunities to follow Jesus' example will not be as literal. It is related that when Hull House was at the height of its renown an English gentleman came to visit and was housed overnight in a guest-room. Late that evening Jane Addams, founder and director of this pioneer social settlement, came down the corridor. Outside his door, in the Continental expectancy that some menial would shine them during the night hours, the visitor had placed his shoes. But Hull House had no such menial. So Miss Addams quietly picked up the shoes, stained with gluey Chicago mud, took them to her room, polished them to a brilliant shine, and returned them to their spot outside the door. No one would ever have known except that years later she was tattled on by another guest who had witnessed the incident. Is not shoeshining a modern equivalent of foot-washing?

Indeed is not any menial task done spontaneously for someone else also the equivalent? In her book, *Erika and the*

King, Erika Leuchtag tells us about her career as physical therapist for the King of Nepal: "As I sat in the garden one day with the princesses a scorpion walked jerkily from the flower bed, its tail held over its head like an umbrella. The princesses ran from it in a quick rustle of silk, but I took off my high-heeled shoe and pursued the insect into a drain, killing it there. I was trying to replace the shoe, standing on one leg and staggering a little, when the King came. He said nothing, but he knelt on the flagstones beside me, took my foot in one hand and put my shoe on it. This would be a natural action in a Westerner, and for that unremarkable. But the King was a Kashatria, the second-highest caste of Hindus. The earth and the feet were the defiling province of the sweeper caste." A king showing servanthood!

Did the disciples learn these lessons Jesus taught them about the saintliness of servanthood? Did they learn to subdue their self-conceit with self-abnegation and deeds of quiet service to the least of the brethren? There is little evidence that they did, at least till after the resurrection. Then in spite of the fact that they were thrust willy-nilly into positions of top leadership in the infant church a great reversal took place. They began to behave as those who serve. Let us see how this came about.

III. The Result

Thus far we have examined the leading characteristics of Jesus' disciples as revealed in the Gospel record. Over all it is not a happy picture. We have also considered how Jesus, detecting a potential for growth sufficient for his needs, taught those disciples basic lessons to hasten their spiritual maturity, lessons which ultimately took root and came to flower. Let us now look in detail at this flowering.

A. The Gospel Record

1. John records the moment when the disciples first ap-

peared to have crossed the divide from self-centeredness to
obedience, skepticism to faith, hopelessness to joy. "Late in
the evening of Resurrection Day, when the disciples were
behind locked doors because of their fear of the authorities,
Jesus appeared among them. 'Peace be with you,' he said, and
showed them his hands and side. Knowing that it was indeed
the Lord, the disciples were filled with joy" (Jn.20:19,20). It was
about time! And from that moment of wholehearted acceptance of the resurrection, the disciples began to mature spiritually into the persons Jesus had seen they could become.

2. Luke confirms this emergence of the disciples from
their "lower natures." He narrates the excitement of the two
men from Emmaus as they tell the Eleven in Jerusalem that
they had entertained the Risen Christ in their home. "While
they were still talking about these marvels, Jesus himself appeared among them. Supposing that he was a ghost, they
pulled back from him in fright." (This was right after two
eyewitness accounts that he was alive!) "Jesus said, 'Why are
you so upset and confused? You can see from my hands and
feet that it is really I. Touch me and see, for ghosts do not have
flesh and blood as I do.' And because they were still incoher-
ent with joy and wonder, he spoke again, 'Do you have anything to eat?' " (Lk.24:36-43).

Then wonder and joy replaced fear; certainty that it was
Jesus replaced doubt. This faith in him enabled them to accept the commission Jesus was ready to give them. For after
he had eaten the fish they offered he said, " 'The things I told
you when I was still with you about everything written concerning me in the Law of Moses and in the Prophets and
Psalms have now been fulfilled.' Then he explained the Scriptures to them, saying, 'Here is what is written — that the Messiah was foreordained to suffer death and to rise from the
dead on the third day, and that there must be a worldwide
proclamation of penitence and forgiveness of sins in his
name, beginning at Jerusalem. Because you have seen these

things for yourselves, I am conferring on you my Father's promised gift. Remain here in Jerusalem till you have been filled with power from on high'" (Lk.24:44-49).

3. This promise of the Holy Spirit to assist them in their spiritual growth and future ministry is also recorded by John in the familiar words: "The Comforter, the Holy Spirit whom the Father will send in my name, will teach you everything, and will keep fresh in your minds everything I have taught you" (Jn.14:26).

Thus it is the indubitable fact of the resurrection, hammered home so many times and then certified by the Holy Spirit, that effected so stupendous a change in the disciples — from dogged unbelief to acceptance of Jesus as their living commander in the new phase of the Kingdom Crusade to which they were committed. John records Jesus as saying to the authorities, "'Destroy this temple, and I will build it again in three days....' But the temple he was talking about was his body. After his resurrection the disciples remembered what he had said, and believed" (Jn.2:19,21,22). Their long tortuous growth upward out of mental rigidity into teachableness, out of self-centeredness into obedience, out of self-distrust into self-confidence — this growth was stimulated and matured by their greater growth out of doubt into faith.

B. Evidence from Acts

A quick look at the Book of Acts provides more than enough documentation for this growth. In the opening chapter Luke reminds Theophilus that after the resurrection Jesus made numerous appearances to the disciples through a forty-day period, instructing them to wait in Jerusalem for the promised baptism of the Holy Spirit. This event finally occurred fifty days after the first Easter, on the morning of the Jewish Feast of Pentecost when the disciples were gathered in the temple for prayer. The Spirit so exalted them that they began to "speak in tongues" — a strange and life-shaking ex-

perience for them. In order to disprove the onlookers' rau-
cous charge that they were all drunk, Peter began an explanation which, through the power of the Spirit within him, became the world's first Christian sermon, and resulted in the
founding of the First Christian Church of Jerusalem, with
3,000 charter members!

No longer were the disciples inclined to mark time, to lie
low or to soft-pedal their faith. Jesus' promise had been fulfilled. They had received the power they needed to carry on
boldly, in the public gaze and under the Establishment's nose,
the work of God's Kingdom entrusted to them by their risen
Lord. These Eleven, nine of whom had not dared to emerge
from hiding between the events of Gethsemane and Joseph's
Garden, were now preaching with great effectiveness the
good news of the resurrection (Acts4:33); they were praying
daily in the temple and enjoying the pleasure of eating in one
another's homes. "And every day the Lord increased the
number of converts" (Acts2:46,47).

Later in the account the disciples were arrested and jailed
by the high priest on the charge of continuing to preach the
resurrection in defiance of orders to "cease and desist." But
"an angel of the Lord unlocked the cell doors and led them
out, saying, 'Go back to the temple and explain the good news
to everyone'" (Acts5:20). The next morning the temple guards
rounded them up again and brought them before the Sanhedrin, a sort of Senate and Supreme Court combined. But this
Council did not dare to do anything drastic because the disciples "were highly regarded by all the people" (Acts2:47). So the
disciples were admonished not to speak about Jesus. To help
the warning sink in, the authorities also had them flogged.

Peter and John had already spent a night in jail for healing
a cripple in Jesus' name but had been released unharmed. So
this incident was the disciples' first rough-handling by the
Establishment. A month earlier they might have heeded the
warning and separated to their own homes, rubbing their
stripes and bemoaning the death of an impossible vision. Not

so on this day! Luke declares that "they left the Council rejoicing that they had deserved the honor of suffering persecution for Jesus' name. And daily they continued in the temple and in people's homes, sharing the good news that Jesus was the Messiah" (Acts5:41,42). The crucial words are "continuing" and "rejoicing"—continuity and joy in proclaiming, through the power of the Holy Spirit, the resurrection and its meaning for everyone, everywhere. Here are two vital reasons for the success of the Apostolic Church.

There have been times in Christian history when the tides of faith have run low. How often those periods of weakness have coincided with the neglect or the discounting of the central ingredient of faith, the Risen Christ! The resurrection was the most important cause for the emergence of the disciples into world prominence. The coming of the Holy Spirit provided the power by which they founded the church and gave their lives in its nurture. Many serious students of the faith suggest that today Christianity may be well into another Dark Age of doubt. In a day when humankind is supersensitive to scientific outlook and discipline, not only the cross, but also the resurrection and the Holy Spirit are "stumbling blocks." This will be true for anyone who does not know the Risen Christ. "Separated from me," Jesus warned, "you are helpless" (Jn.15:5). But when he comes into our midst and we acknowledge that it is indeed he, then what has hitherto been incredible will become bedrock certainty. Like the disciples of old, we will move out from enervating doubt into enabling faith. And when enough individuals have this experience, the present encroaching darkness will begin to recede.

Of all the disciples, Peter shows most strikingly the change produced by a growth in faith. As we now look at each of the disciples individually, how appropriate it is to begin with the man who rose to be their leader.

Chapter Two

Peter
The Metamorphosed

I. The Parable of Ableman's Quarry

A few miles from the Dells of the Wisconsin River stands Ableman's Quarry. It is a huge cavity excavated from the roots of an ancient mountain system. From it have been taken hundreds of thousands of tons of buff-colored quartzite for use in the building trades and road construction. The rock is layered not horizontally, as with most rock, but in almost a true vertical. As one looks at the rock face and runs his hand over it, he thinks, "Why, it has ripple marks, just as sand does along the edge of a lake." And that is right, for the mountain stump rearing up impressively before him was, millions of years ago, the level bottom of a shallow inland sea. The continuous action of waves left its marks on the successive layers being washed in from surrounding higher land, till the thickness of this ripple-marked sand reached several thousands of feet. It continued as a soft sedimentary deposit for many thousands of years.

But there came a time of revolution, when pressure and heat were brought to bear on those flat layers of soft sand. Gradually they were metamorphosed first into sandstone and then into tough quartzite. Yet they retained the watermarks of their original deposition. Through the diastrophic convulsion of mountain making these layers were slowly buckled, much as ribbon candy is shaped, into a tremendous mountain chain, with the old flat surfaces being forced into an upright position. Thus an interesting chapter in the mighty story of creation may be read from the strata in this quarry.

Here is a parable of Jesus' Number One disciple, Simon Peter. His life reflects a similar diastrophic revolution which changed him from the irresponsible horizontal of shifting beach sand to the stalwart vertical of solid quartzite. He began life with Jesus as Simon the Sandlike, but he became Peter the Rocklike. But to state this now is like disclosing how a plot of a novel is concluded before the opening chapters have been read. In order to understand the dimensions of the radical revolution in his life we must start where the Gospel records begin.

The Gospel according to Mark is probably the closest to Peter's own autobiography that we have. Papias, Bishop of Hierapolis, one of the early Church Fathers, about the year 130 A.D. wrote: "John the Elder used to say this also: Mark became the interpreter, and wrote down accurately everything that Peter related of the sayings and doings of Christ.... Thus Mark made no mistake when he thus wrote down some things as Peter remembered them." Thus had Simon Peter done nothing else than provide the basic material for the earliest story of Jesus, it would have been more than sufficient to keep his memory green. For this Gospel is so distinctive and impressive a type of literature that when Matthew's and Luke's Gospels appeared some ten and fifteen years later respectively, they revealed their indebtedness by using Mark's chronology, and by incorporating with their own material more than three-quarters of Mark's material almost word-for-word. We owe a considerable debt of gratitude to Simon Peter as an inspired source of the earliest Gospel.

II. Simon the Sandlike

The story of Simon the Sandlike opens with John the Baptizer appearing in the wilderness, "preaching a baptism of repentance for the forgiveness of sins" (Mk.1:4 RSV). It became the popular thing to hear him, for he even attracted Jerusalemites. Those who were penitent were baptized by him in the Jordan River as they confessed their sins. It was natural that so dynamic a personality as John should attract disciples, and John's Gospel informs us that one of those was Andrew the Fisherman. Andrew probably was present when the wilderness prophet baptized Jesus, so that Jesus first met Andrew on that occasion. Then through Andrew, Jesus became acquainted with the fisherman's brother, Simon. Nothing issued from this contact at once, because after receiving baptism Jesus returned to his Nazareth shop where he remained till John the Baptizer was arrested.

A. His Call

When Jesus learned of the imprisonment of John, who was his first cousin, he left Nazareth and came into Galilee to continue the work John had been forced to abandon. "The time is fulfilled, and the Kingdom of God is at hand," he declared. "Repent, and believe in the good news" (Mk.1:14,15 RSV). People flocked to him in such numbers that he realized he would be needing help. "As he stood one day on the shore of Lake Gennesaret the people, in their eagerness to hear the word of God, crowded him back to the water's edge. He noticed two empty fishing boats on the beach nearby, whose owners were rinsing their nets in the shallow water. Stepping to the nearest boat he asked Simon, the owner, to push a few feet out into the water. When he was seated in it, he continued teaching the crowds along the shore.

"When he was through he said to Simon, 'Shove out into deep water and let down your nets for a catch.'

"Simon replied, 'Andrew and I were out all night, Master, and never caught a thing. But because you ask it, I will let down the nets.' On doing so, they enclosed so huge a school of fish that their nets began to snap. They cried to their companions in the other boat to come to their aid and soon both boats were filled with fish almost to the danger-point.

"When Simon Peter realized what had occurred, he dropped to his knees before Jesus and exclaimed, 'Have nothing to do with me, Lord, for I am a sinner!' For both he and his partners James and John, who were Zebedee's sons, were overawed by the catch they had made.

"But Jesus replied, 'Simon, do not be afraid. From now on you will be after a different kind of catch—men!'

"And when they had brought their boats safely to land they abandoned everything and followed him" (Lk.5:1-11).

B. His Background

What do we know about Simon? He was the son of Jona (John) and a native of Bethsaida, later moving to Capernaum where he and his brother Andrew became fishing partners of Zebedee's boys. He was a property-owner who had hired help, which put him in the middle class. When he later exclaimed to Jesus, "Look, we have abandoned everything to follow you!" (Mk.10:28), he was not speaking rhetorically but factually, for the two sets of brothers had given up a lucrative business. He probably knew Greek in addition to the Aramaic he spoke, and had been taught to read the Scriptures in Hebrew. Although lacking a formal education such as Paul had enjoyed, Simon was not just an ignorant fisherman. He was the only one of the Twelve identified as being married (although Paul in I Cor.9:5 hints that some of the others may have been and states that Simon's wife accompanied him on his journeys). Clement of Alexandria reports her name to be Perpetua, states that she bore children, and that she was crucified at the same time as her husband.

What were Simon's personal qualities? The answer depends on what period of his life we examine—before or after Jesus' death. The various accounts indicate that he was the most forthright disciple of them all, and the most fickle. He was the most virile and the most vacillating. He was the most impressive and the most impulsive, the most perceptive and the most obtuse. He was a complex and contradictory figure, at first one whom Jesus almost despaired of (Lk.22:31,32), but finally one whom people revered (Ac.5:15). However, as the records explicitly reveal, he began by being Simon the Sandlike.

C. His Characterization

The words of a Negro Spiritual describe Simon the Sandlike as he is revealed in the Gospel record:

> Sometimes I'm up, sometimes I'm down, O yes, Lord,
> Sometimes I'm almost to the groun', O yes, Lord.

The dynamics of Simon's personality were pendulum-like, swinging rapidly from one extreme to another. His motivations and concerns oscillated between self-centeredness and unselfishness. Impetuosity and impulsiveness warred continuously with prudence and caution. Or, to use a vertical simile, his faith traced a roller-coaster-like track across his life, one moment breathlessly climbing the heights, the next plunging sickeningly in a descent to the depths. Five examples may illustrate the shifting-sands behavior which characterized Simon's pre-resurrection life.

1. Perceptivity versus Instability

A. Luke reports that one day Jesus said to his disciples, "'It is inevitable that an individual will sometimes stumble morally. But woe be to him who is the cause of it. It would be better for him to be dropped in the ocean with a millstone around his neck, than to lead one of these little ones into wrongdoing. So keep a strict watch over your own behavior. If your brother wrongs you, rebuke him; and if he repents, forgive him. If he wrongs you seven times in succession, and each time seeks you out and says, "I'm sorry," you must forgive him.'

"The apostles said to the Lord, 'Make our faith bigger!'" (Lk.17:3-5). Now, Simon had been growing into a larger understanding of his Master's motives and purposes than had the others. He had revealed this in a shrewd question which he had put to Jesus, who had just told the Parable of the Watchful Servants. Simon had asked, "Is this parable aimed just at us, or is it for everyone?" (Lk.12:35-41). So now, after listening to Jesus teach about forgiveness, he posed this question: "Master, if my brother keeps doing evil things to me, how many times shall I forgive him? More than seven times?" (Mt.18:21).

"Look, Lord," he seemed to be saying, "I listened to you back there when you said that we should forgive seven times. I know it's hard, but if a fellow could manage that many, might he go a bit further and stretch it to fourteen times?" He was learning to take Jesus' teaching with more than literal faithfulness, looking deeply into its spirit and trying to make that spirit his own.

"Jesus replied, 'I tell you not just seven times, but seventy times seven!'" (Mt.18:22). This stands for an infinite number of times. Computers are not to warn us when the number 489 comes around. We are to put no limits on our practice of forgiveness, partly because of its possible effect on others, and partly because of its possible effect on us.

Because Simon asked this searching question, Jesus told the magnificent parable which confronts us with the uncomfortable truth that if we expect to receive forgiveness, we must practice it (Mt.18:23-35). Thus Simon demonstrated a spiritual perceptivity which set him apart from the other disciples.

But this perceptivity is balanced by the spiritual insensitivity which Mark records. After a heavy day of teaching and healing, Jesus knew that his spiritual capital was in need of replenishment. So "early the next morning, long before dawn, he arose and sought a secluded spot to pray. Simon and the others searched for him, and when they had found him Simon said. 'Everyone is looking for you!'" (Mk.1:35-38). There are strong overtones of irritation in that statement. The disci-

ples had searched in many places and were tired and hot.
Simon voiced the exasperation of them all, saying in effect,
"Lord, what on earth are you doing in this God-forsaken spot?
Big crowds have come to hear you today, and you're off hiding in the hills! Let's get the show on the road! There's nothing to be done for the Kingdom in this place. Come on back
and tell the people about the Kingdom!"

Obviously, this occurred before Jesus revealed his solvent
system of spiritual strength, and may have been the incident
which caused him to share that secret with them. Whatever
the enterprise, input must equal outgo, or bankruptcy results.

Ignace Paderewski wrote in his autobiography that when
he skipped practicing one day, he noticed the difference. If he
missed practicing two days, his critics noticed the difference.
And if he skipped practicing three days, his audiences knew
it.

There is a French proverb: "What is seen is important, but
what is not seen is essential." — in this case, the hidden labor
which lies behind accomplishment.

Dr. Harry Emerson Fosdick once told a visiting group of
seminary students, "For every minute I preach, I spend one
hour in preparation."

Simon lacked the sensitivity to understand this law of the
spiritual life.

B. We read in John another example of Simon's occasional
flashing insight. Jesus had been using metaphors to explain
his mission. "When the crowd heard him say, 'I am the Bread
which came down from heaven,' many began to mutter de-
rogatory things about him. 'Why, this is Jesus, the son of
Joseph,' they said, 'and we know both of his parents. He can't
fool us by saying, "I have come down from heaven"'" (Jn.6:41,42).

"Jesus replied, 'I am the Bread of Life. Your forefathers,
indeed, ate manna in the wilderness, and they eventually
died. But there is another kind of bread, also coming down

from heaven, which a man may eat and live! I am that living Bread. Whoever eats of this Bread will live forever, and the Bread which I give for the life of the world is my own flesh' (Jn.6:48-51).

"On hearing him say this, many of his followers exclaimed, 'This is more than I can accept. No one can possibly believe all that!' (Jn.6:60).

"From that time on, therefore, numbers of them deserted him and returned home. Jesus said to the Twelve, 'Will you desert me, too?'

"Simon Peter replied, 'Lord, who else is there to go to? What you say bears the stamp of the eternal. We know with certainty that you are the Holy One of God!'" (Jn.6:66-69).

A bold statement for impetuous Simon to make! It marks his upward growth toward the insight required of the one who was destined to head the infant Christian Church.

But then came one of the most exalted adventures of Simon's life. It was literally a mountaintop experience, occurring according to tradition on the slopes of Mount Hermon, which at once both awed and frightened him. Luke relates that Jesus "led Peter and John and James up into the hills to pray. As he prayed, the divine radiance touched him, so that his features were transfigured and his clothes became blindingly white. All at once there appeared two men, Moses and Elijah, similarly radiant, who talked with him about his forthcoming death in Jerusalem. Peter and the others had been sound asleep, but they suddenly awoke and saw what was happening.

"Just as the men began to leave, Peter exclaimed to Jesus, 'Master, how good it is to be here!' Then, without realizing what he was saying, he blurted, 'Let's build three shrines here—one for you, one for Moses, and one for Elijah!'

"The words were no sooner spoken than a cloud began to overshadow them, making them afraid. As it settled down around them, there came a voice from it, saying, 'This is my Son, my Chosen One; pay attention to what he says!'

"And when the voice ceased, Jesus was alone again" (Lk.9:28-36).

Now Simon did not acquit himself well. For one thing, although Jesus had begun to include him in his quiet periods of prayer, Simon had not been busy praying. The record baldly states that he was sleeping—perhaps practicing for Gethsemane! So when he awoke, he found himself in the midst of something he sensed was of tremendous significance—but he could not identify it. He knew that whenever the Patriarchs had known a mystical encounter with the Almighty they had erected a monument to preserve its memory. Jacob did so at Peniel (Gn.32:30) and Samuel at Ebenezer (I.Sam.7:12), so it seemed fitting to Simon that similar shrines should now be built for the three radiant figures, in order to perpetuate the wonder of the event which was taking place before his eyes. So he blurted out this patriarchal proposal.

Now Jesus might have said, "Why, Simon, that is a good idea! This has been a key experience for me. It establishes my credentials to lead the Kingdom Crusade. Sure, let's preserve my Transfiguration experience through shrines to which everyone in the nation will want to pay homage!" This would have linked him to the historic Establishment, which predated that of Annas and Caiaphas, and would have shown that he had the approval of two of the Founding Fathers.

But Jesus showed no enthusiasm for Simon's impulsive suggestion. Why not? Three reasons may have been uppermost in his mind:

1) "No one puts new wine into old wineskins" (Mk.2:22).

2) He had stated, "My kingship is not of this world" (Jn.18:36 RSV). That is, while it is to occur on earth and for the benefit of all people, that kingdom will depend not so much on religious institutions, holy places, and established rites and rituals as it will depend on people's feelings and thoughts, inten-

tions and deeds. To go through the proper rites at a Christian shrine does not make one a Christian. Jesus' true followers are not those who are content with observing prescribed rituals at prescribed places. Rather, they are those who give him first place in their total living. Perhaps Jesus believed that there were enough wood-and-stone shrines in his country already, and that what was required of his disciples was that they enshrine his spirit within their hearts.

3) Jesus also knew that one can occasionally climb to a mountaintop, but that one can rarely stay there. Peaks are only for short-time enjoyment and long-time memory.

My wife and I once stayed for some days in the village of Steckelberg in the Bernese Oberland in Switzerland. It lies at the head of the Lauterbrunnen valley, and one may hike up a switchback trail to Muerren some two thousand feet above, and see the alpine villages of Grindelwald and Kleine Schadegg lying just under the mighty rampart of the Jungfrau. From Muerren one can ascend by cable car to the summit of the Schilthorn — bleak, snow-covered and half-shrouded in cloud. The trip up is a pleasure but, weather permitting, the view is superlatively enjoyable. As night falls, however, the cable cars stop running and one must return to Muerren.

Life is lived not on the peaks, but on the lower slopes and down in the valleys. It is not on the summits where the Kingdom of God is to be found, but rather,

"Where cross the crowded ways of life,
    Where sound the cries of race and clan."

This latter reason was underscored when the four came down the mountain to the village at its foot. There they found a small crowd, at the center of which were the disciples who had stayed behind. They were frustrated and ashamed at having failed to heal an epileptic boy.

To climb a mountain can be a memorable adventure, for

we can make the ascent over and over again in memory. Similarly, to attain some spiritual summit can also be memorable, for we can relive it in our hearts while our feet are taking valley paths. Personal quest may drive us to a mountaintop, but the Kingdom Crusade urges us down again. For example, Jacob could not remain in the desert where he had wrestled with God; he had to go on to be reconciled with his brother. Isaiah could not continue in the temple after his vision; he had fifty years of work to do among his people. The Bethlehem shepherds could not stay forever in the stable, any more than could Jesus. A minister cannot maintain the holy glow induced by a dozen ordaining hands on his head, for no sooner is the service over than some petty soul bustles up to complain that the organ was too loud. But everyone who has climbed to a mountaintop experience can come down in the company of the God whom he met up there, and who will then walk with him along the various roads of everyday living.

C. The alternating moods of Simon's perceptivity are nowhere more strikingly revealed than in Matthew's record of his recognition of Jesus' true significance. "On coming into the region near Caesarea Philippi Jesus asked his disciples, 'Who do people say that the Son of Man is?'" He was sounding them out regarding his popularity, by asking with whom he was being identified.

"'Some say that you are John the Baptizer,' they replied. 'But others say Elijah, and still others Jeremiah or one of the other prophets.'"

Jesus' next question revealed how deep his concern was: "'But who do *you* say I am?'"

Here was a totally different question, putting the disciples on the spot, requiring them to yield their innermost thoughts. As his enemies grew bolder Jesus had to depend more and more on his disciples. Now was the time to find out how dependable they were, how well they had accepted his claims, how committed they were to him and to his Kingdom Crusade. Up to this point they had been hedging, not quite willing to accept Jesus as Master of all humanity. So he was pushing them toward a moment of decision and an act of commitment when he asked, "What is your opinion of me?"

Here it was that Simon reached the loftiest moment of perceptivity. While the others sought in their minds for an acceptable reply which would not fully commit them, the true answer instantly flashed into Simon's mind, and he made his ringing commitment: "You are the Messiah! You are the Son of the living God!"

With these words he was the first to declare publicly what Christendom has affirmed for twenty centuries. Simon the Sandlike was beginning his metamorphosis into quartzite. No wonder he became the bishop of the first church!

"'What a fortunate man you are, Simon, son of Jonah,' replied Jesus. 'You did not learn this from human sources but by revelation from my Father. And I will also tell you that you are Peter the Rock. It is on such rocklike faith as this that I will found my church so securely that the powers of death shall not overwhelm it. I will give you the keys to the Kingdom of Heaven. Whatever you forbid on earth will be forbidden in heaven, and whatever you permit on earth will be permitted in heaven.' Then he commanded the disciples to tell no one that he was the Messiah" (Mt.16:13-20).

"What is your opinion of me?" This question has been faced not only by the twelve disciples, but also by every individual in every century who has been attracted to the Christian Way. Each modern disciple is confronted with the demand that he acknowledge the divine credentials of Jesus. Christianity cannot survive on half-faith.

How Simon's heart must have been "strangely warmed" by Jesus' words of commendation for his perceptivity. He must have welcomed, also, the new Aramaic name of Cephas, rendered Peter in Greek, which means "rock." Simon the

Sandlike was no appropriate name for a disciple! "Peter the
Rocklike" was much more desirable! "Sometimes I'm up,
sometimes I'm down" — and now Peter was up. And he stood
just a little straighter.

D. But unfortunately, true to his nature, he slipped down
almost immediately into a mood of spiritual insensitivity. He
couldn't stay on his mountaintop, but he neglected to bring
back with him his newly-found gift. Mark records that some
of the harshest words Jesus ever spoke to a disciple were now
directed at Simon Peter.

The text says that "From that day forward Jesus began
to teach his disciples the need for going to Jerusalem. There
he would suffer at the hands of the elders, the Chief Priests
and the scribes, would die and three days later be restored to
life" (Mt.16:21).

Such words must have rocked the disciples back on their
heels. Once again it was Peter who first recovered and spoke
in impetuous contradiction. He who in the previous inning
had hit the second pitch right out of the park, now picked up
his big bat once more and stepped to the plate, for we read:
"Peter seized Jesus' arm and took him to task, saying, 'God
forbid! This must never happen to you, Lord!'" (Mt.16:22).

"Why, Master," he was saying in effect, "that's a lot of non-
sense! Why are you talking about suffering and dying when
glory is waiting for you? You are God's Chosen One, and such
ideas are ridiculous!" Poor Simon! His first words as the
newly-christened Peter showed none of the perceptiveness
expected of "the Rocklike!"

What despair must have been in Jesus' heart, for he
turned and said to Peter, "Get out of my sight, you Satan! You
are an obstacle in my path because you think not as God
thinks, but the way men do" (Mt.16:23). The recent home run
hitter had struck out!

How Peter must have cringed under this stinging rebuke!
Undoubtedly he was also bewildered, for he had spoken im-

petuously out of a deep concern for Jesus' safety which he deemed essential to the survival of the Kingdom Crusade. Obviously he had understood only half the meaning of the Messiahship which he had acknowledged at Caesarea Philippi—its divine origin. The other half, its human destiny, was wholly different from the garden-variety of Jewish belief. Jesus was saying in effect to Peter, "You have been thinking like everyone else who wants to be freed from the tyranny of Rome. Like Simon the Zealot and Judas Iscariot, you are expecting me to be a second Judas Maccabeus to drive the Romans into the sea. But the Messiah whom God has sent in my person is not a militant one based on physical violence. Rather he is to be a suffering servant as visualized by Isaiah, who offers a compelling, irresistible example of conduct which can modify human behavior. My Father's world, which he yearns for us to enjoy in place of the one we have shaped, is built not on violence but on love. We ally ourselves to this fundamental force of love when our major concern for others is not to get the better of them, or to ignore them or even to smash them, but rather to will them every good thing which my Father makes available to those who serve Him."

It is related that a few days after Abraham Lincoln had delivered his Second Inaugural Address, promising "to bind up the nation's wounds" (including those of the South) "to care for him who shall have borne the battle, and for his widow and orphan—to do all which may achieve and cherish a just and a lasting peace," a woman who had lost a son at Gettysburg accosted him and said bitterly, "You should not be coddling our enemies, Mr. President. You should be destroying them."

Lincoln replied gently, "Madam, do I not destroy my enemies when I make them into friends?"

"Not by might nor by power but by my Spirit, saith the Lord of hosts!" (Zech.4:6 RSV) is the Old Testament parallel.

But Jesus did not stop when he had thus rebuked Peter.

There followed a teaching which might not have been spoken
but for Peter's obtuseness. "Then Jesus said to them all,
'Whoever would become my disciple must give up all claim to
self and follow me, accepting whatever cross may result. For
the one who hoards his life will impoverish it, whereas the
one who freely spends his life on my behalf will enrich it"
(Mt.16:24,25).

This challenge to total discipleship still exists today. In
The Nun's Story, Kathryn Hulme translates the demands of
Christlike commitment into the conditions of hospital nursing. The mother superior in charge of the hospital introduced
the neophyte nurses to their ward duties with these words:
"All for Jesus ... Say it, my dear students, every time you are
called upon for what seems to be an impossible task. Then
you can do anything with serenity ... Say it for the bedpans
you carry, for the old incontinents you bathe, for those
sputum-cups of the tubercular." Then as she deftly changed a
terminal patient's foul-smelling dressings, she added, "You
see how easy? All for Jesus. This is no beggar's body picked
up in the Rue des Radis. This is the Body of Christ and this
suppurating sore is one of his Wounds."

Without as much drama but with equal intensity Jesus
challenged his volatile disciples, using Peter's insensitivity to
enrich our understanding of discipleship.

2. Thermal Instability

Peter oscillated between the opposite poles of insight and
insensitivity. But his faith also alternated between glowing
ardor and frigid unbelief. Let us examine two illustrations of
this "thermal instability."

a) Matthew tells us that Peter's faith once turned from
cold to hot and then back to cold again, all within sixty sec-
onds. At sundown after a strenuous day, Jesus sent the disciples by boat to another part of Lake Galilee while he took the
shore path to the rendezvous by himself. Finding along the

way a quiet place, he stopped for the meditation and prayer which alone could sustain him through the arduous demands of the morrow. Meanwhile, beset by contrary winds, the boat carrying the disciples had difficulty making headway to the spot where they were to meet Jesus. Matthew declares that about 3 A.M. he came toward them walking on the lake. The disciples, of course, were terrified at the sight and cried out, "Look! A ghost!"

Jesus called to them above the storm, "Do not be afraid. I am no ghost."

Peter was the first to recover from his fear. Finding his tongue, he cried impulsively, "If it be truly you, Lord, tell me to come to you!"

"Very well," replied Jesus. "Come!"

With a characteristic upsurge of faith Peter climbed over the gunwale and walked on the water toward his Master. But suddenly becoming aware of the enormity of his gamble, the depth of the water beneath his feet, the violence of the wind and the consequent physical danger to which he had subjected himself impetuously, he found his faith collapsing like a punctured rubber duck. Beginning to sink, he shrieked in desperation, "Lord, save me!"

At once Jesus reached out and caught him by the hand, asking, "Why did you doubt me, O man of little faith?" (Mt.14:27-33).

When they were safely in the boat, it is likely that Peter was ashamed of the mercurial fluctuations his faith had gone through — trembling fear, soaring confidence, abysmal terror, and a strong sense of security. But does this not show how human he was! Does this experience of his not parallel that of every disciple of Jesus everywhere? How easy it is to have great resolves of heart, and how hard it is to find that we cannot sustain the glow which produced them! How simple it is for us, having been stirred by some rousing spiritual impulse, to venture forth on some bold crusade which will put our faith to the test; and how difficult it is, once we have left the security of our haven and feel the full opposition of wind and wave, to hold our course in the face of what could be mortal danger!

Archbishop Cranmer found it relatively easy to guide England's shift from the Roman to the Anglican Church, as long as Henry VIII and Edward VI supported him. During those years he wrote much of the stately and inspiring liturgical prose of the Book of Common Prayer. But within three years after "Bloody Mary," a loyal Roman Catholic, had succeeded to the throne, Cranmer found himself at the center of a raging storm. Indeed, he was buffeted by so many waves and billows—being convicted of treason and heresy, being excommunicated from the church, and being condemned to death—that in confusion and despair he sought to outride the storm by repudiating his Protestant faith. This hope proved to be futile, for Mary had personal reasons for wanting him dead. But Cranmer's faith, beset as it had been by thermal instability, had one more rising. When he had been tied to the stake and the faggots had been lighted, he was asked to affirm publicly his submission to Rome, and so discredit the English branch of the Reformation. Instead, Cranmer raised his right hand and exclaimed in bitter contrition, "This is the hand that signed the recantation. It shall be the first part of me to burn!" And he thrust it firmly into the leaping flames. A heroic rebirth of faith which must never be forgotten!

b) Peter's see-sawing, his blowing cold and then hot in faith, is also plain in the 13th chapter of John, in a scene which has endeared the impulsive disciple to Christians of every age and nation.

"Knowing that the Father had given everything into his keeping, and that he had come from God and would return to God, Jesus arose from the supper table. He took off his outer clothes and wrapped a towel around his waist. Then he poured water into a basin and began to wash the disciples' feet, drying them with the towel" (Jn.3:3-5).

Simon's flash-point being low, the disciple was immediately indignant that his Lord and Master should be acting like the commonest slave. Here was an affront to the Messianic dignity! This feeling was amplified by Simon's inner knowledge that he did not deserve such treatment at the hands of Jesus anyway, because he was such a poor follower.

Simon Peter reminds me of an Indian on a reservation who was asked by a tourist what he did for a living. "I'm a preacher," came the laconic reply.

"Oh," the visitor continued. "Do you mind telling me how much salary you get?"

"Fifty dollar a month."

"Why," exclaimed the tourist, "that's pretty poor pay!"

The Indian shrugged. "Me pretty poor preacher!"

Is it not likely that Simon was feeling rather much like that Indian? So when his turn came, he exclaimed in disbelief, "'You're actually going to wash my feet?'"

"'You may not understand now what I am doing,' Jesus replied, 'but some day you will.'

"Simon cried, 'I will never let you wash my feet!'

"'If I do not wash you," Jesus said, 'you may no longer share my life'" (Jn.13:6-8).

To the astonished disciple this sounded like an ultimatum, and so it was. Jesus was teaching his disciples by deed as well as word that his messiahship was not kingliness but servanthood. There was to be no new Establishment of pomp and ceremony, prestige and power; rather there was to be a warm fellowship of those who serve in Jesus' name. Jesus knew that if Peter did not grasp the idea this night at this final supper, he might forever be lost to the Kingdom Crusade. "Simon," he said in effect, "if you do not accept this act of service from me, and accept what it signifies, you are refusing to continue in my work. Our mission is to serve the last and the least of men."

It was a tense situation — an inflexible Master facing the impetuous disciple. Who would yield?

His faith blowing hot again, Simon knew with a great flash of inward clarity that the most important fact was that he must be wholly a part of Jesus' mission. Nothing else could satisfy this man who would soon be metamorphosing from disciple into leader. So bowing his head in complete submission he said intensely, "'Then not just my feet, Lord, but also my hands and my head!'" (Jn.13:9). In this symbolic act he was saying in effect, "Let the whole of me be involved. Wash me completely!"

When William Booth was asked the secret of his success in founding and leading the Salvation Army in its difficult early years, he said quietly, "It was because God had all there was of William Booth."

Nothing less than a one hundred percent surrender can suffice. "Wash not just my feet, Lord, but all of me!"

D. The Denials

Peter's vacillation came to a climax in the events of Maunday Thursday night. At the table Jesus had just told his disciples that his time with them was short and that soon he would be leaving them. "Peter said to him, 'Just where are you going, Lord?'

"'Where I am going,' Jesus replied, 'you are not now able to go. But you shall follow me later.'

"Peter said to him, 'Why can't I follow you now, Lord? I am ready to give my life for you.'" And he really meant it.

"'Will you indeed give your life for me?' Jesus answered. 'It is the solemn truth that before cock-crow you will have denied me three times'" (Jn.15:36-38).

How did Peter feel when his earnest declaration of utmost

loyalty was brushed aside with a prophecy that he would act in just the opposite way? John does not tell us, but Mark and Luke give us these parallel accounts:

"After singing a hymn they went out to the Mount of Olives. There Jesus said to them, 'Tonight the faith you have in me will be shattered. For the Scriptures say, "I will strike down the herder and the sheep will be scattered." Yet after I have been raised I will go ahead of you into Galilee.'

"Peter exclaimed, 'Everyone else may lose faith in you, but I won't' (Mk.14:27-29).

"'Simon, Simon, listen! Satan wants to seize you and sift you like wheat. But I have prayed for you, that your faith may not falter, and that when you have withstood the test, you will freely share your strength with your brothers.'

"'Lord,'Peter protested, 'I am willing to go with you either to prison or to death' (Lk.22:31-33).

"'I tell you, Peter,' returned Jesus, 'that this very night, before the cock has crowed twice, you will deny me three times.'

"Peter then repeated even more emphatically, 'Even if I must die with you, I will never deny you.' And everyone else said the same thing" (Mk.14:29-31).

But how poorly Peter and the others lived up to their promises is a matter of unhappy record. Mark tells us: "On coming to a spot named Gethsemane Jesus said to them, 'Stay here while I pray,' and took Peter, James and John on farther with him. When fears began to torment him and distress to weigh heavily on him, he said to the three, 'My anguish is more than I can bear; wait here and keep alert.' Then he went farther on yet, dropped to the ground and prayed that if possible, he might be spared the dangers of the hour. 'Abba, Father,' he said, 'to You all things are possible; therefore take this cup from me. Nevertheless, let not what I want, but what You want, be done.'

"He came again and found the three disciples asleep. He

said to Peter, 'Could you not keep awake for just one hour? Stay awake now, and pray that you will not be put to the test. Your spirit is willing but your body is weak'" (Mk.14:32-38).

How ashamed and embarrassed the three must have been! Jesus' body needed sleep as much as Peter's, but Jesus was faced with a decision which involved his very life. Peter, however, was not sensitive enough to Jesus' inward turmoil to offer the empathetic understanding which his Master needed. Had Peter made an authentic effort to share Jesus' desperate vigil and be supportive in this crisis, sleepiness would have been no problem. The three disciples may have been only fifty feet away from Jesus' kneeling figure, but they were a thousand miles from his praying soul. Thus, because Peter was not experiencing the emotions which were tearing at Jesus, there was little to keep him awake.

The record continues: "Jesus went away again to pray, using the same words. And when he returned, he found that they had not been able to keep their eyes open, and were sleeping again; and they could offer him no excuse" (Mk.14:39,40).

How might they have acted differently? Well, they could have followed their Master's example and prayed. But this is no easy thing to do when one is tired.

A woman once said to me, "When I can't get to sleep, I start praying for everyone I know. Long before I have finished the list I am asleep!" But this was not prayer so much as it was simple medication! She should have taken Sominex instead, and prayed during the daytime! For prayer is neither a sleeping-potion nor chinking for life's empty places. Authentic praying demands the full concentration of all faculties, which in turn produces spiritual alertness.

At an Ocean Park, Maine, Rural Life Conference in 1940, a refugee from the ruins of Warsaw told of her family's efforts to survive. Once each day, from the relative security of the basement of their destroyed home, one of the men slipped out to forage through the wrecked city for food. Danger was ever-present for the searcher, but never greater than when he had found something and was on his way home, for others would kill to possess it. Meanwhile, the rest of the family prayed, from the moment he left the shelter till the moment he returned; and then they offered a prayer of gratitude. "And we never felt that we had truly prayed," said Mrs. Benedict, "unless we had broken out in sweat."

Thus Peter and the others might have exhausted themselves praying for Jesus — and stayed awake in the bargain — but apparently it did not occur to them. They had not yet learned the full dimensions of prayer.

> Because I've resolved to add prayer to my life,
> She'll not be my mistress: I'll make her my wife!
> >   For just as my honesty can't be downgraded
> >   To "policy" which, in a pinch, is evaded,
> So also my praying in mind and in heart
> Roots deeper than simply a "practice" or "art."
> >   To offer just sections of me is a fraud —
> >   I'll wager the whole of myself on God.

It is related that a young nun had scarcely begun her life in a convent when she was stricken with tuberculosis. When the sister superior came to see her in isolation, the nun burst into tears. "I feel so awful," she exclaimed. "I'm just a drag on everyone here. My particular responsibilities must now be piled on everyone else — and each of them has enough to do as it is. There's nothing that I can do to help for a whole year."

"But there is," said the sister superior softly.

The young woman looked at her wide-eyed.

The older woman nodded. "Yes. You can pray! Spend the time in prayer which you ordinarily would have devoted to your regular round of duties, and you will be helping God lend strength to us all. And it may be, also, that God in his great mercy will shorten your illness."

Peter and the others, however, lacked this spiritual insight. Thus when Jesus came yet a third time he exclaimed, "Are you still asleep and taking it easy? So be it. My hour has come, for the Son of Man has been betrayed into the hands of evil men" (Mk.14:41).

Thus in those hours when Peter might have been stoking his faith to make it red-hot for any contingency, it was cooling down, and was therefore ineffectual.

Earlier in the Upper Room, following his prophecy of Peter's denials, Jesus advised the rest to sell their cloak and buy a sword. "'Look, Lord,' they replied, 'we have two already!'"

"Jesus said to them, 'They are enough'" (Lk.22:36,38).

This is a curious passage. Were the swords to be used to protect him from arrest? Was Jesus considering, after all, the use of violence? Would two swords, or a sword for each of them, have been of any effect against Roman soldiers? Is it not likely that Jesus' words were ironic, because in the Garden he explicitly repudiated the use of force? When Jesus was arrested, "Peter, having a sword, drew it and slashed at Malchus, the servant of the high priest, severing his right ear. Jesus said to Peter, 'Put your sword back into its scabbard. Must I not drink the cup which my Father has set before me?'" (Jn.18:10,11).

Impetuous Peter! He would show Jesus how unwarranted were those ugly forecasts of his denials! But unused to a weapon, and failing to select a proper tactical target such as a priest or centurion, he swung blindly and almost missed.

Once in a game of Bible Baseball I pitched this question at the batter: "What is the source of the passage, 'First the blade, then the ear'?" I expected him to reply that it was from Jesus' parable of the seed growing secretly, Mark 4:28.

He paused for a moment, his brow furrowed in thought. Then he smiled and exclaimed, "Peter in the Garden!" It was indeed! And what a ridiculous figure Peter made!

Matthew continues the account from his own special source: "Jesus said to his defender, 'Put your sword back into its scabbard, for all who wield the sword will die by the sword. Do you not suppose that I can appeal to my Father? Why, he would send more than twelve legions of angels to my defense! But how then could the Scriptures come true which state that these events must take place?'" (Mt.26:52-54). And Luke adds, "And he touched the servant's ear and healed him" (Lk.22:51).

By now the coals of Peter's faith were beginning to blacken. This rebuke drained from him all the vigor with which he had swung the sword, and the fight went out of him. So when "all the disciples deserted Jesus and took to their heels" (Mt.26:56), very likely Peter was in the lead.

But when he was safely away and out of breath, impetuous Peter began to have second thoughts. His running away could be construed as a denial, and this idea he could not tolerate. So, feeling ashamed and very likely still afraid, he crept back to watch Jesus being tied and marched off to the high priest's palace. Luke describes the disciple's reaction delicately: "But Peter followed afar off" (Lk.22:54 KJV). He tagged along closely enough to see what was happening, but far enough back to be safe. In doing so, he provided an example for all too many future disciples — people who follow Jesus at a distance, free from direct personal involvement or any embarrassing commitment. In contrast to the "pillars" of a church who support it from the inside, they are "flying-buttresses" who support it strictly from the outside. Although there were many such in Jesus' time, the two most renowned were Nicodemus, a Pharisee and member of the Sanhedrin, and Joseph of Arimathea. One showed up only at night, and the other after Jesus was dead! Would Jesus' fate have been any different if influential men like these had vigorously and visibly given him their support?

Now the stage was set for the predicted denials. "For

when Jesus was taken inside the palace courtyard, Peter summoned enough courage to follow. But as he slipped through the gate, the woman stationed there said to him, 'Aren't you one of the prisoner's disciples?'

"'I am not!' Peter replied.

"Because it was cold, the servants and guards had built a charcoal fire about which they gathered for warmth. Peter finally joined them in order to keep warm.

"Now while Peter was warming himself someone said to him, 'Aren't you one of his disciples?'

"'I am not!' he stated flatly.

"Then one of the high priest's servants, a relative of the man whose ear Peter had cut off, said, 'Didn't I see you with him in the garden?'

"Just as he denied it again, the cock crowed" (Jn.18:17,18,25-27). And Luke adds that across the courtyard, "the Lord turned and gave Peter a searching look. Then Peter remembered how Jesus had told him, 'Before the cock crows twice, you will deny me three times.' And he went out and wept bitterly" (Lk.22:61,62).

Peter had hit bottom. Heroic intentions had lost out to cowardly denial. His self-image in small pieces about him, he recognized that Jesus had known him better than he knew himself. This knowledge plunged him into the depths of despondency.

In an autobiographical bit, Harper Jensen states, "For some years I lived to the devil's glory. Then, because God is not mocked, I slipped down and down till one day I was out, and bitterly aware of it. Fortunately I wasn't face down, but flat on my back, and so found myself looking up. It came to me that I should get my body to following my eyes. No helping hands from relatives or friends were in sight to give me a boost upward. But out of my childhood there came echoing into mind a Sunday School memory verse: "He who believes in me, though he die, yet shall he live." Now, I had died — I was lying there stone-cold dead in sin. But suddenly here was promise of new life through believing in Jesus. And my new hunger to live again — this time to God's glory — brought me up on my feet again. Jesus' words were true. I have experienced resurrection through faith."

Peter, too, was rescued through faith. But did his courage come back quickly enough for him to be present at the crucifixion, as was John? The Gospels make no mention of his being there. But Peter himself, in his First Letter, intimates that he was: "So I exhort the elders among you, as a fellow-elder and a witness of the sufferings of Christ as well as a partaker in the glory that is to be revealed" (1 Pe.5:1 RSV). And if his courage was on the rise again, so was his faith.

As one considers these many shameful events, he is impressed by Peter's humanness — how much like almost everybody else he is! For what person does not "get hot" about whatever stirs him most deeply, and then gradually "cool off" as the inspiration fades? We have our high moments and our low, even though much of the time we are "in between on the misty flats." But Peter was more honest than most people in the facing of personal weakness, because the time came when he publicly acknowledged that he had indeed been Simon the Sandlike. Much of our information about his barometric variances comes directly from his own testimony. It was he who laid bare many of these incidents in the hope, perhaps, that other disciples who were threatened with a similar vacillation might take fresh courage. Peter was heartened to do this because by that time he was no longer Simon the Sandlike, but Peter the Rocklike.

For with the crucifixion and resurrection of Jesus, Simon began to pass through a personal revolution analagous to the mountain-making upheaval in Wisconsin which metamorphosed soft sand into hard quartzite. Just precisely how this

was accomplished within Simon we do not know, except that
central to his metamorphosis were two factors: (1) He finally
accepted Jesus' resurrection unequivocably; (2) he was baptized at Pentecost by the Holy Spirit. The period of metamorphosis through which the Ableman Quarry sand was hard-
ened into rock was millions of years in duration, but Simon
was changed into Peter in less than fifty days — the time from
Easter to Pentecost. We learn about the new person he was
becoming by reviewing the Gospel record of the appearances
of the risen Jesus, then the Acts of the Apostles, Paul's references and ancient tradition.

III. Metamorphosis:
The Post-Resurrection
Appearances

Peter stands foremost among the disciples in many accounts of Jesus' appearances following his resurrection. Paul
is the authority for the belief that the Master revealed himself
to Peter before any of the others. "For I delivered to you as of
first importance," he wrote to the Christians in Corinth,
"what I also received, that Christ died for our sins in accordance with the Scriptures, that he was buried, that he was
raised on the third day in accordance with the Scriptures,
and that he appeared to Cephas, then to the Twelve. Then he
appeared to more than five hundred brethren at one time,
most of whom are still alive, although some have fallen
asleep. Then he appeared to James, then to all the apostles.
Last of all, as to one untimely born, he appeared also to me" (1
Cor.15:3-8 RSV).

Each of the Gospels has something distinctive to tell us
about the various post-resurrection appearances. Mark relates that when the two Marys and Salome went to the tomb
to anoint Jesus' body, a young man dressed in white robes
told them, "'Do not be astonished. You are looking for Jesus of

Nazareth who was crucified. He is not here because he is risen. Look, here is the place where they laid him. But go to his disciples and Peter and tell them that he has gone ahead into Galilee where you will see him, just as he told you'" (Mk.16:6,7). The angel singled out Peter for special mention — an early intimation of Peter's growing leadership.

John relates that Mary Magdalene went early to the tomb and found the stone rolled away. At once she made off to tell Peter and John. "They both ran, but the other disciple outran Peter and reached the tomb first; and stooping to look in, he saw the linen cloths lying there, but he did not go in. Then Simon Peter came, following him, and he went into the tomb; he saw the linen cloths lying, and the napkin which had been on his head, not lying with the linen cloths, but rolled up in a place by itself. Then the other disciple, who reached the tomb first, also went in, and he saw and believed" (Jn.20:4-8 RSV).

When I was six, during the course of an uninspired afternoon, my playmate Frank brightened things up considerably by suggesting that we turn in a false fire alarm. I set off running at full speed to the alarm box at our corner. Breathless, I arrived at the box ahead of Frank. As I waited for him to come puffing up, the glamour of the adventure began to dissipate, and I looked up at the red box with growing uneasiness. Suddenly I had visions of a monstrous fire engine bearing down menacingly upon me, disgorging helmeted and rain-clad men with fierce visages, who advanced on me with up-raised axes. So I drew back and said, "Frank, I don't think I want …."

"Sissy!" he exclaimed happily, and shinned up the pole till he could reach the little dangling hammer. He smashed the glass and pulled down the lever, setting off signals in the Fire Station up by Fairbanks, Morse and Company. I looked at him in horror, and fled to my refuge under our back porch. In my original enthusiasm I had reached the alarm box first, but then began to have second thoughts. Beginning to be frightened, I backed off and left it to Frank to complete the project. Both of our names, however, were in the newspaper.

John was the faster runner, but his courage failed him. Thus it was Peter who led the way into the tomb to discover that his Master was indeed gone. He was learning to change his impetuosity from an obstacle to faith into an instrument of faith.

On another occasion, following Jesus' instructions, the disciples had gone to Galilee and were waiting with some degree of impatience for word from their risen Lord. Seven of them were together on the shore of the Sea of Galilee. After watching the fishing-boats nostalgically, Peter impulsively exclaimed, "I'm going fishing!" and the others eagerly joined him. They went out that night but had no luck.

"Just as day was breaking Jesus stood on the beach; yet the disciples did not know it was Jesus. He said to them, 'Children, have you any fish?'

"They answered him, 'No.'

"He said to them, 'Cast the net on the right side of the boat, and you will find some.' So they cast it, and they were not able to haul it in, for the quantity of fish.

"That disciple whom Jesus loved said to Peter, 'It is the Lord!'

"When Simon Peter heard that it was the Lord, he put on his clothes, for he was stripped for work, and sprang into the sea" (Jn.21:4-7 RSV).

It was John who first recognized Jesus, but it was Peter who impetuously plunged into the water and swam the hundred yards to shore. He could not endure the slower pace of the boat, but wanted to be reunited immediately with his Master.

In that same encounter with Jesus, Peter received his personal commission. With it went a warning that martyrdom would be his pay for its acceptance. For when they had eaten a breakfast of bread and fish, which surely must have re-minded them of the feeding of the five thousand, and the supper in the Upper Room, Jesus turned to the one who was emerging as his foremost disciple. Looking him squarely in the eyes, Jesus said, "'Simon, son of John, do you love me above all things?'

"Peter replied, 'Yes, Lord, you know how I love you.'

"Jesus said, 'Feed my lambs.'

"A second time he asked, 'Simon, son of John, do you love me?'

"'Yes, Lord,' Peter replied, 'you know how I love you.'

"Jesus said, 'Care for my sheep.'

"Then for a third time he asked, 'Simon, son of John, do you really love me?'

"Peter was hurt that Jesus had put the same question yet again, and exclaimed, 'Lord, you know everything, so you know that I really do love you.'

"'Then feed my sheep,' replied Jesus" (Jn.21:15-17).

Here is a challenge to haunt every ordained individual in the church, and every lay person who believes that he or she holds a ministry under Christ! It points directly toward the fundamental task of our commitment. There are so many things which a church is expected to do today that some-times we get our priorities in disarray. Then it is we need to be reminded that the primary task before us is found in three words: "Feed my sheep."

A parenthetical bit of pastoral widsom was derived from this passage by a salty old minister who said in my hearing, "Yes, Jesus charged me to care diligently for both his sheep and lambs. But somehow he never mentioned what to do about the old goats—both billies and nannies—whch often infest his flocks. So I've always felt that there was an open season on them. Many's the time I've had to heave one over the back fence!"

But directly following Peter's commissioning came Jesus'

warning: "Solemnly I tell you that when you were young you dressed and went wherever you wanted to; but when you are old you will stretch out your arms, and someone else will tie you up and carry you where you do not want to go." Thus Jesus foretold the kind of death by which Peter would glorify God. Then he added, "Follow me!" (Jn.21:18,19).

And from that moment on Peter did follow him, faithful to death. The Kingdom Crusade had its new leader.

IV. Peter the Rocklike

Paul states that Peter had been entrusted with the Gospel for the Jews (Gal.2:7), signifying that he had become God's choice to carry forward the work which Jesus had so reluctantly relinquished. Four incidents from the Book of the Acts confirm this fact and indicate the way in which Simon the Sandlike continued to metamorphose into Peter the Rocklike. They showed how the perceptive and courageous things he did brought him into leadership within the small group of believers.

A. Assumption of Leadership

1. First, Peter initiated the action to fill the place among the original disciples left vacant by the death of Judas.

The number "twelve" and its multiples had both a historic significance and a personal meaning to the disciples. The fifth of the seven numbers Jews held sacred, stemming originally from the Twelve Patriarchs, its value was enhanced by various Old Testament usages. In addition, for many months the disciples had been a tightly-knit band of a dozen men engaged in a religious crusade. Now with the defection of Judas, their holy unity as a Twelve was broken, and they deeply felt its loss. Peter in particular sensed that the symbolic and comtemporary meanings ought to be restored, so that the disciples could think with warmth and satisfaction, "Now we are Twelve again."

The disciples agreed, and elected Matthias to the position.

2. At Pentecost Peter was the leader of the apostolic band at the founding of the world's oldest church, the First Christian Church of Jerusalem. He also delivered the first Christian sermon, thus launching the great apostolic proclamation of the Good News of Christ. It came about in this way.

Having been persuaded by his several appearances to them that Jesus had indeed risen from death, the disciples had returned to the Upper Room where they had stayed earlier, to await the fulfilment of his promise that they would receive power from God. Accordingly they devoted themselves to prayer in the hope that the Holy Spirit might soon appear. They were together as usual on the morning of Pentecost, an ancient Jewish Feast, when suddenly the room was filled with a sound from heaven like the rushing of a mighty wind. Looking about in astonishment and fear, the disciples saw "tongues as of fire" resting on each of them, filling them with the long-awaited Spirit. Under the influence of this impelling power each one began to speak ecstatically as the Spirit led them. Because the festival had attracted to Jerusalem many Jews residing in other countries, the crowd which gathered included persons who spoke a variety of languages. The record states that they were astonished to hear their own language spoken by Galileans, and they cried, "What's going on here?" Some wag in the crowd, making no sense of the outbreak, guffawed a cynical reply: "Ho! They're brimful of new wine! That's what!" The initials "D.D." mean "Doctor of Divinity"; but on a police blotter they stand for "Drunk and Disorderly." The onlookers had some difficulty in distinguishing between the two.

This was more than Peter could bear. He got to his feet and cried boldly, "You are wrong! These people are not drunk. When did you ever see a drunken crowd at nine o'clock in the morning?" Having thus gained their attention, Peter began a hard-hitting sermon proclaiming the Good News about Jesus.

"Men of Israel, hear these words: Jesus of Nazareth, a man attested to you by God with mighty works and wonders and signs which God did through him in your midst as you your- selves know — this Jesus, delivered up according to the defi- nite plan and foreknowledge of God, you crucified and killed by the hands of lawless men. But God raised him up, having loosed the pangs of death, because it was not possible for him to be held by it." And Peter concluded with the uncom- promising words, "Let all the house of Israel therefore know assuredly that God has made him both Lord and Christ, this Jesus whom you crucified!" (Ac.2:22-24,36 RSV). Daring words!

But these words had carried conviction, for the record continues that the listeners were "cut to the heart, and said to Peter and the rest of the apostles, 'Brethren, what shall we do?'

"Peter said to them, 'Repent, and be baptized every one of you in the name of Jesus Christ for the forgiveness of your sins; and you shall receive the gift of the Holy Spirit.'" About three thousand responded to this first altar call, "and they devoted themselves to the apostles' teachings and fellowship, to the breaking of bread and the prayers" (Ac.2:37,38,42 RSV).

What would have happened that morning if Peter had in fact been drunk, or could not summon courage to seize so magnificent an opportunity? Would the Christian Church not have been founded, or would God have had to use another of the disciples to bring it alive? This is needless speculation, because Peter did respond with inspired courage and psy- chological skill. He was no longer Simon the Sandlike; he was becoming Quartzite Peter. From a human perspective, it is because of his forceful presentation of the claims of Christ that we today observe Pentecost as the Church's birthday.

3. Peter resumed Jesus' healing ministry. Peter and John had gone to the temple to pray, and had been accosted for alms by a lame man at the Beautiful Gate. "Peter directed his gaze at him, with John, and said, 'Look at us.' And he fixed his

attention upon them, expecting to receive something from them.

"But Peter said, 'I have no silver and gold, but I give you what I have; in the name of Jesus Christ of Nazareth, walk.' And he took him by the right hand and raised him up; and immediately his feet and ankles were made strong. And leaping up he stood and walked and entered the temple with them, leaping and praising God" (Ac.3:4-8 RSV).

This naturally attracted a crowd. Impulsively seizing the opportunity, Peter preached his second sermon since Pentecost and won the loyalty of about five thousand of his listeners.

4. Accepting arrest, Peter faced the full power of the religious Establishment with a boldness which members of the young church copied.

After this healing, before they could leave the temple, the two disciples were arrested by the temple guards and kept in prison overnight. When they were haled before the high priests, the elders and the scribes, they were asked, "By what power or in what name did you work this miracle?"

One can almost hear electricity crackle as Peter stood and replied with sledge-hammer blows: "Rulers of the people and elders, if we are being examined today concerning a good deed done to a cripple, by what means this man has been healed, be it known to you all, and to all the people of Israel, that by the name of Jesus Christ of Nazareth, whom you crucified, whom God raised from the dead, by him this man is standing before you well."

Up till now the Establishment apparently had not realized who these prisoners were. For the record continues: "Now when they saw the boldness of Peter and John, and perceived that they were uneducated, common men, they wondered; and they recognized that they had been with Jesus" (Ac.4:8-10 RSV).

What are the "marks" which Jesus lays on those who follow him faithfully, as a testimony that they have been with him? When the renowned missionary and explorer, David Livingstone, died in Chitambo in the heart of Africa, the natives buried his heart near the village. After preserving his body, they bore it reverently to the coast where it was placed on a steamer and sent to England to be interred in Westminster Abbey. But some congenital nitwit asked if the casket actually did enclose Livingstone's body, or if the black natives had perpetrated a ghastly hoax on the British Empire. The matter was debated with great heat till a friend of the missionary who was a doctor examined the remains and declared authoritatively, "This is David Livingstone's body. It bears identifiable marks of his African experience. There, for example, is the hand that was crushed by the lion that attacked him. The bones have knitted, but the damage is still visible."

But there were more than the marks of a lion on Dr. Livingstone. To his severely plain tomb there should be added these words: "I bear on my body the marks of Jesus" (Gal.6:17 RSV). What better epitaph could there be? The badges of true apostleship are not like sheriff's stars, to be pinned on a vest till the next election. Nor are they like gowns and hoods for one-time graduation exercises, or Sunday-go-to-meeting clothes to be put on for special religious occasions. Rather, the marks of Christ, by which an individual is identified as having been with him, are found within life at every homely moment: in the eyes that kindle with sympathy, that grow warm with kindliness or that flash with holy indignation on another's behalf; in the voice that gives quiet counsel to the confused, offers friendliness to the lonely, encourages the downcast, bears witness to faith in God and brotherliness through Jesus; in the hands that heal, steady, sustain and offer themselves continuously in deeds of loving service.

To flesh out this list with a bill of particulars would make a diverting and profitable Sunday afternoon occupation, especially if those engaged in the quest would conclude by asking themselves, "How many of these marks do I bear?"

The Jerusalem authorities recognized, of course, that they had no grounds for punitive action against the two. But wanting to put a scare into them, they said, "We're going to let you go. But you will be in trouble again — deep trouble — unless you stop all teaching and healing in the name of this man Jesus!"

But Peter replied, "You have demanded that we listen to you rather than to God. But as for us, we must continue to tell others what we have seen and heard."

It was inevitable, then, as the new sect continued to grow and the name of Jesus was heard everywhere in the streets, that the high priest had all the disciples thrown into prison. "But at night an angel of the Lord opened the prison doors and brought them out and said, 'Go and stand in the temple and speak to the people all the words of this Life'" (Ac.5:19 RSV). The next morning they were arrested again. The high priest said to them sternly, "'We strictly charged you not to teach in this name, yet here you have filled Jerusalem with your teaching and you intend to bring this man's blood upon us.'

"But Peter and the apostles answered, 'We must obey God rather than men. The God of our fathers raised Jesus whom you killed by hanging him on a tree. God exalted him to his right hand as Leader and Savior, to give repentance to Israel and forgiveness of sins. And we are witness to these things, and so is the Holy Spirit whom God has given to those who obey him'" (Ac.5:28-32 RSV). This decision to give God first rights to human obedience was not a new stance in the world's moral history. The ancient Greek playwright Sophocles dealt with it in "Antigone." Her brother has been a traitor to the city-state, has been executed and then left unburied as a warning to others. Stating that "there is a law of love deeper than the shame of treachery, and higher than the law of the state," Antigone gives the body a decent burial. She is arrested and the magistrate asks why she had dared to disobey the law. She replies courageously:

> I did not dream thine edicts strong enough
> That thou, a mortal man, should'st overpass
> The unwritten laws of God and know no change.

But her words are unavailing, and she is sentenced to death by starvation.

Likewise, the high priest and Council naturally wanted to handle the disciples "with extreme prejudice"! Here was deliberate defiance of their treasured authority by a group of Galileans led by the same two men they had had trouble with before. This was mutiny! It was a rebellion against the divine right of Establishments! Such a treasonable movement must be crushed before its toxins infected the hearts of the common people. Thus when Martin Luther proclaimed, "Here I stand. I cannot do otherwise. My conscience is captive to the will of God," and publicly burned the Papal Bull of his excommunication, Frederick the Elector had to take him into protective custody to save him from the Roman Establishment.

Four hundred and twenty years later another German theologian, Karl Barth, was forced to make a similar choice. When he was required to give approval to the Nazi-inspired German Aryan Church, he replied, "What I have to say in this matter is simple — I say no, without reservation or qualification. It is the business of the church to serve the Word of God." He was dismissed from his position in Bonn University, and found refuge in the University of Basel in Switzerland.

In 1660 a poor tinker named John Bunyan was thrown in jail for preaching without a license. Told that he would be turned loose if he promised to stop preaching, Bunyan replied hardily, "If I were out of prison today, I would preach the Gospel again tomorrow, by the help of God!"

The courage of these men, faced with Peter's predicament, would have warmed the cockles of the saint's heart! Doubtless he would have approved the way in which Chief Justice Charles Evans Hughes of the United States Supreme Court summarized Peter's words, "We must obey God rather than men": "Much has been said of the paramount duty to the State, a duty to be recognized, it is urged, even though it conflicts with convictions of duty to God. Undoubtedly that duty to the State exists within the domains of power, for government may enforce obedience to laws regardless of scruples ... But in the forum of conscience, duty to a moral power high than the state has always been maintained .... One cannot speak of religious liberty without assuming the existence of a belief in supreme allegiance to the will of God."

How did the disciples fare? The priests and Council, who believed that they represented God's will, were eventually persuaded to let the apostles go. The man who achieved this remarkable feat was a rabbi and liberal-minded Pharisee named Gamaliel. A grandson of the renowned Hillel, he had also served as Paul's tutor. "If just men are behind this movement," he counseled, "it will collapse of its own accord, and you will be rid of such men as these. But if God is behind it, not only will you be powerless against them, but you will also be guilty of fighting against God himself!" (Ac.5:34-39 RSV).

Gamaliel held the scholar's view of history. God's mills may produce some unusual products, but they are still his mills. This scholar was stating a variant of the old adage, "Time will tell." The months, the years and the centuries support the moral order: "Time wounds all heels!" Time has a disconcerting way of winnowing chaff from grain, falsehood from truth, men's desires from God's will. Only what is of the same stuff as God's universe ultimately survives. History may be regarded in part as the story of what happens both to people whose ideas conform to the moral structure of the cosmos, and to people whose ideas do not so conform. Time has certified the claims of Jesus, which have survived the severest testings which twenty long centuries have been able to offer.

So the apostles were warned again to keep quiet about Jesus. That the warning might sink in more deeply and make them more compliant, they were also beaten before being released. Then Luke writes two of the most memorable sentences in the New Testament. Peter and John and the others "left the presence of the Council, rejoicing that they were counted worthy to suffer dishonor for the name. And every day in the temple and at home they did not cease teaching and preaching Jesus as the Christ" (Ac.5:41,42 RSV).

They left the courthouse rejoicing! One would expect them to slink out, rubbing their smarting backs and muttering about police brutality. But they were rejoicing, so the record assures us, because they had been beaten. It scarely seems possible, till one ponders the testimony of the German philosopher, Johann Fichte, who wrote: "A good conscience is the ground of joy."

And a good conscience the disciples most certainly had! Sometimes one hears the phrase, "pure unadulterated happiness." Yet to the thoughtful follower of Jesus is there really such a thing? Ian MacLaren did not think so, for he once exclaimed, "The highest joy to the Christian almost always comes through suffering. No flower can bloom in paradise which is not transplanted from Gethsemane." Trouble appears to be the springboard by which one attains the highest joy. Here is a paradox which is the very stuff of our faith!

B. Ananias and Sapphira

By the time of the unhappy encounter with Ananias and Sapphira, Peter's leadership seems to have been accepted by everyone in Jerusalem. Nowhere does the record suggest that Peter ever politicked to win it. Rather he simply reacted to each situation as he was impelled to. Because each of his actions appeared to be right, the other disciples followed his lead by common consent.

By now there had grown among Jesus' followers a strong brotherly bond in which each contributed as he was able to the welfare of all. Some students of this brief period have incautiously labeled it as a time of "early church communism." In terms of the communism we know today, such a label is patently ridiculous. Rather, it was merely an earlier version of Captain John Smith's dictum in the little colony of Jamestown: "From each according to his ability; to each according to his need." The record states: "There was not a needy person among them, for as many as were possessors of lands or houses sold them, and brought the proceeds of what was sold and laid it at the apostles' feet; and distribution was made to each as any had need" (Ac.4:34-35 RSV).

Then occurred an event which may have resulted in the end of this brotherly practice. The late Jess Norenberg, one-time superintendent of the Wisconsin Congregational Conference, once related a traumatic experience of his childhood. His mother had baked a small pudding for supper and set it to cool on a windowsill overlooking the street. Having a ten-year-old's insatiable appetite and flexible morals, he stole off with the pudding and ate it.

At supper-time when the disappearance was reported, the children were asked if they knew anything about it. His heart thumping, little Jess shook his head. His mother finally concluded that a passing tramp had made off with it, and the boy's pulse slowed down to a normal beat. But not for long. It was their custom to close the evening meal with a reading from the Scriptures. Reaching back for the family bible on the buffet behind him, Father Norenberg opened to the fifth chapter of Acts and began reading: "But a man named Ananias with his wife Sapphira sold a piece of property, and with his wife's knowledge he kept back some of the proceeds, and brought only a part and laid it at the apostles' feet."

Ironically the name Ananias means "The Lord has been gracious."

"But Peter said, 'Ananias, why has Satan filled your heart to lie to the Holy Spirit and to keep back part of the proceeds of your land? While it remained unsold, did it not remain your own? And after it was sold, was it not at your disposal? How is it you have contrived this deed in your heart? You have lied not to men but to God.'

"When Anaias heard these words, he fell down and died. And great fear came upon all who heard of it. The young men rose and wrapped him up and carried him out and buried him."

Little Jess sat at the supper table paralyzed by fear. Would young men be coming to bury him, too?

Either innocently or mercilessly, Father Norenberg continued the reading: "After an interval of about three hours his wife came in, not knowing what had happened. And Peter said to her, 'Tell me whether you sold the land for so much.' And she said, 'Yes, for so much.'

"But Peter said to her, 'How is it that you have agreed together to tempt the Spirit of the Lord? Hark, the feet of those who have buried your husband are at the door, and they will carry you out.'

"Immediately she fell down at his feet and died. When the young men came in, they found her dead, and they carried her out and buried her beside her husband. And great fear came upon the whole church, and upon all who heard of these things" (Ac.5:1-11 RSV).

And great fear also increased in little Jess. "All that evening," he recalled, "I sat on the davenport listening for the feet of the young men." And no one in the family was observant enough to give him the needed reassurance.

Some people have regarded this Scripture account as an ugly blot on Peter's reputation. They assume that he possessed lethal power — "Bang! Bang! You're both dead!" — and had used it irresponsibly on people who should only have been rebuked. But this is a misreading of the account. Peter was no avenging angel, no Joshua confronting Achan. Ananias and Sapphira did not die because he had sentenced them to that fate. In some way he had learned about the deceit and confronted Ananias with it. He pointed out that it was not men who were being cheated, but the Holy Spirit. Peter may have been astonished when he thus triggered Ananias' heart attack; but it sounds as though he assumed that guilt would also carry off Sapphira with a stroke! However we may interpret this part of the event; however we tend to view it through twentieth century eyes, the results, whatever their cause, seem to be much too severe for the crime.

Yet how contemporary Ananias is! In today's world, would not an audit of his Federal Income Tax report have caused him acute embarrassment?

When the Internal Revenue Service telephoned a church to find out if John Jones had given $500 to the church as he had claimed, there was silence for a moment; then the minister replied, "He will! He will!"

The pastor of a wealthy church once remarked cynically to me, "If everyone who cheated on his income tax were to drop dead, I suspect that my church would be decimated!"

Ananias' sin consisted of wanting more credit than he deserved. He had a right, as Peter pointed out, to "contribute to the necessities of the saints" only as much as he wanted, and to keep the rest for himself and his wife. But he and his wife wanted to be known not as tithers but as give-all-ers and thus bask in the undeserved esteem of the brethren. It is not astonishing then, that this man's name is preserved only in "Ananias Clubs," where amateur and professional liars gather

for sport! (Such usage dishonors the name of another
Ananias, however — the man who sought out the blinded Paul
in Damascus, restored his sight and baptized him into the
Christian faith.)

That Peter did not become an ogre in the eyes of the
people because of the death of this couple is shown by the
fact that the infant church continued to grow. "More than
ever, believers were added to the Lord, multitudes of both
men and women, so that they even carried out the sick into
the streets, and laid them on beds and pallets, that as Peter
came by, at least his shadow might fall on them. The people
also gathered from the towns around Jerusalem, bringing the
sick and those afflicted with unclean spirits, and they were
all healed" (Ac.5:14-15 RSV).

C. Peter As Church President

The death of Stephen triggered the first full-scale drive of
the Establishment against the thriving church. "On that day a
great persecution arose against the church in Jerusalem; and
they were all scattered throughout the region of Judea and
Samaria, except the apostles. Devout men buried Stephen,
and made great lamentation over him. But Saul laid waste the
church, and entering house after house, he dragged off men
and women and committed them to prison" (Ac.8:1-3 RSV).

It was as though a bomb had gone off in the midst of the
congregation, blowing them far and wide into the country.
But wherever they fled they made new converts and established new congregations. It became Peter's duty and opportunity, then, to oversee these young churches. He began
traveling among them, bringing them counsel and inspiration
and, wherever needed, correction or rebuke. In addition to
these administrative responsibilities he also carried on his
healing ministry, curing a paralytic named Aeneas and restor-
ing Dorcas to life.

While in Caesarea he had a vision that the Gentiles were also to become part of the Christian enterprise. The vision centered around a Roman Centurion of the Italian cohort, a religious man who with all his household reverenced God, praying continually and giving generously to the needy. Peter sought him out, discovered that Cornelius had had a similar vision, and told him of the Good News of Christ. He began by saying, "Truly, I perceive that God shows no partiality, but in every nation any one who fears him and does what is right is acceptable to him."

While he was speaking, the Holy Spirit came upon them all. Amazed, Peter exclaimed with all his old impetuosity, 'Can any one forbid water for baptizing these people who have received the Holy Spirit just as we have?' And he commanded them to be baptized" (Ac.10:34-48 RSV).

When he returned to Jerusalem, Peter found that he had to defend his unprecedented action. He told the rest of the disciples the whole story, and concluded by saying, "'If then God gave the same gift to them as he did to us when we believed in the Lord Jesus Christ, who was I that I could withstand God?'

"And they glorified God, saying, 'Then to the Gentiles also God has granted repentance unto life'" (Ac.11:17,18 RSV).

Thus Peter pioneered in establishing a climate that would inevitably produce the great missionary thrust which was ultimately responsible for the spread of Christianity around the globe. Had he still been Simon the Sandlike, would he not have rejected the vision, told Cornelius that the admission of Gentiles to the church was much too controversial, and cut off all further debate! Then the parallel missionary work in which Paul was engaged might have been lopped off the church, and both parts might have died. True enough, Paul reports that Peter once backslid from this decision some years later, so that when they met in Antioch Paul had to take

him to task severely (Gal.2:11f). But Luke reports that after this
confrontation Peter held true to his worldwide vision—fortunately for us today—and swayed the apostles and elders to
this point of view. Had Peter gone parochial yet again, we
might, in Rockwell Harmon Potter's picturesque words, "still
be quarreling for acorns under the oak trees of northern
Europe!"

Before the Scriptures closed the account of Peter the
Rocklike, King Herod declared war on the church. The different members of this remarkable family, descended from Anti-
pater, are hard to keep separate in mind, but it was Herod
Agrippa I who launched the brief but fierce persecution. "He
killed James the brother of John with the sword; and when he
saw that it pleased the Jews, he proceeded to arrest Peter
also" (Ac.12:2,3 RSV). "President" Peter was chained in a dungeon
between two soldiers. An angel released him and led him to
safety. He reported briefly to John Mark's home to make his
escape known to his friends and then left the city. With this
event the Bible becomes silent about Peter. Whatever else
there is to report comes not from Scripture but from tradition.

As one surveys the biblical records he sees that the key
themes of Peter's leadership are these: the resurrection of
Jesus and his messiahship by the intention of God, the need
for repentance and the forgiveness of sins, and the eventual
triumph of righteousness in a New Age, when "the earth will
be filled with the knowledge of the glory of the Lord, as the
waters cover the sea" (Hab.2:14 RSV). These are also fundamental
tenets of the Christian faith, which must be proclaimed in
every generation.

There are no records earlier than A.D. 170 which confirm
that Peter had ever been in Rome, had headed the church
there or was executed there. No historical certainty underlies
the claim that he was martyred by Nero in the year 64. But
rich traditions come to us from several sources.

Peter still had need of his rocklike faith because Nero had begun a persecution of Christians throughout the Empire. The Roman historian Tacitus states that everyone in Rome believed the great fire of 64 had been set on the orders of the emperor. He continues, "Nero set up as the culprits and punished with the utmost refinement of cruelty a class hated for their abominations, who are commonly called Christians .... Besides being put to death they were made to serve as objects of amusements; they were clad in the hides of beasts and torn to death by dogs; others were crucified, others set on fire to serve to illuminate the night when daylight failed."

There were times when it could hurt to be a Christian. And Peter was to find this out, for tradition as preserved in the Acts of Peter, chapter 35 (written one hundred fifty years after his death), declares that in the full knowledge of his danger Peter journeyed to Rome to hearten the endangered Christian community. As the number of deaths increased, those who remained implored Peter to escape so that his leadership might be spared for other churches who needed him. Under pressure he agreed, and fled down the Appian Way. But he was abruptly halted by a vision of Jesus walking toward the Eternal City.

Peter asked, "Where are you going, Lord?"

Jesus replied, "To Rome, to be crucified there."

Remembering poignantly, as though it were but the day before, how he had once denied and deserted Jesus in his extremity, Peter turned about and went back to share the lot of his fellow-Christians.

Finally he was apprehended and condemned to death. His wife Perpetua was also arrested and condemned to be crucified while Peter watched. Eusebius quotes Clement of Alexandria's account of the disciple's conduct during her martyrdom. "They say that when the blessed Peter saw his own wife led out to die, he rejoiced because of her summons and her return home, called to her very encouragingly, addressing her by name, and saying, 'O, thou, remember the Lord!' All this occurred while his own cross stood waiting. When at last his executioners came for him, Peter made a final request. 'I am not worthy to die as did my Lord,' he said. 'I pray thee, crucify me with my head to the ground.'"

Peter has been gone these many, many years. But he has left us an extremely vivid picture of his life as a disciple and leader, and from it we may take courage. It is easy to be Simon the Sandlike in our own discipleship. But the same power which remade Peter can change you and me — if we will — into the disciples of rock-like faith on which Jesus placed his trust.

Chapter Three

Andrew
The Inconspicuous

ONE of the saints of the Northeast Harbor Union Church in Maine was "Gram" Tracy. To my knowledge she never held office or was awarded any front-line recognition. Essentially a quiet, self-effacing person who may have felt she lacked the aggressive confidence of a "born leader," she kept well in the background of events, within the shadows cast by those who headed the boards and committees and special task-forces. Yet she was quietly part of every effort which the church made for the enrichment of community, nation and world. It was her influence more than the visible leadership of many of the church's elected officers which caused the parish to prosper. Because she was behind every effort, rather than out in front, her value may have gone unnoticed in some areas. This did not trouble her, however, for she was not interested in building a reputation, but only a church.

Gram Tracy came to mind as I reviewed the sparse biblical record of the disciple Andrew. She and the saint of old were spiritually akin. The New Testament suggests that Andrew was not meant for front-line responsibility. Rather, his greatest area of effectiveness lay in his unrecorded relationships within Jesus' Kingdom Crusade. Completely overshadowed as he was by his big brother, Peter, his value lay in what he did behind the scenes — an area generally given no credit.

Let us examine what the New Testament says about him. His name appears in all the listings of the disciples in the Four Gospels and Acts, but the first three Gospels contain absolutely no record of anything he said or did on his own. Every bit of our information as to what he was personally like comes from John's Gospel. The data are easy to review because they are so few, but they do suggest a variety of titles which might fit him.

I. Andrew the First-Called

John tells us that Andrew was Jesus' very first disciple. It came about in this way: "The next day again John (the Baptizer) was standing with two of his disciples; and he looked at Jesus as he walked, and said, 'Behold the Lamb of God!'

"The two disciples heard him say this, and they followed Jesus. Jesus turned and saw them following, and said to them, 'What do you seek?'

"And they said to him, 'Rabbi, where are you staying?'

"He said to them, 'Come and see.'

"They came and saw where he was staying; and they stayed with him that day, for it was about the tenth hour. One of the two who heard John speak and followed him was Andrew, Simon Peter's brother" (Jn.1:35-49 RSV).

On the basis of this passage, Andrew was known in the infant church by the title of "Protokletos," or the First-Called.

II. Andrew the Persuader

The same account relates that Andrew provided Jesus with the disciple destined to become the leader of all, his brother Simon. The record continues that Andrew "found his brother Simon and said to him, 'We have found the Messiah.'

He brought him to Jesus. Jesus looked at him and said, 'So you are Simon, the son of John? You shall be called Cephas' (which means Peter)" (Jn.1:41,42 RSV).

Thus Andrew not only committed himself to the Kingdom Crusade, but also sought to bring his family under the same commitment. It is not astonishing that he was successful in winning his brother, for he and Simon were close to each other. they lived in the same house on the lake near Capernaum, were partners with James and John in a fishing enterprise, and jointly owned the boat which Jesus so frequently used.

Andrew's success in winning his brother so impressed Billy Graham that he has made "Operation Andrew" an integral part of every crusade.

III. Andrew the Sharer

This title is appropriate because the little that is known about him underscores his peculiar ability to enlist the sympathies of others in Jesus' crusade. For Andrew it was obviously not enough to have found the Messiah. He was forever passing on the good news to others so that they might find the joy that was his. By this token he might also have been named "the Evangelist" or "the Missionary," because he knew that he had to keep sharing his faith in order to be worthy to retain it. Two instances may illustrate Andrew's behind-the-scenes activity as a sharer.

A. Andrew and the 5,000

The first is one sentence of only twenty words, the only words of his to be recorded. Yet he is warmly remembered not just because he spoke them, but because of what he thereby revealed of himself. The occasion was perhaps a late afternoon when Jesus was on a hillside by the Sea of Galilee, surrounded by people who had watched him heal the sick and listened to his teaching about the Kingdom of Heaven.

Jesus then had said to Philip, "Where can we buy food for these people to eat?" They were some distance from the nearest "supermarket," and it was nearly closing time anyway.

Philip had shrugged. "Fifty dollars' worth of bread wouldn't be enough, even if everyone had only one piece. And besides, we have no butter!"

But Andrew had already been thinking about the problem, and had been making a quiet investigation. He had discovered that Jesus engaged in neither idle talk nor futile action. His Master was planning something—Andrew did not know what it was—but he did what he could to make everything ready. So he came to Jesus and said, "There is a lad here who has five barley loaves and two fish, but what are they among so many?"

"Jesus said, 'Make the people sit down.'

"Now there was much grass in the place; so the men sat down, in number about five thousand. Jesus then took the loaves, and when he had given thanks, he distributed them to those who were seated; so also the fish, so much as they wanted" (Jn.6:9-11 RSV).

Andrew has earned the right to be called "the Sharer" because he sought out and brought to Jesus the lad whose generosity made the feeding of the 5,000 possible.

B. Andrew and the Greeks

Again, John relates that "among those who had gone up to worship at the festival were certain Greeks. They came to Philip, who was from Bethsaida in Galilee, and said to him, 'Sir, we want to see Jesus'" (Jn.12:20, 21).

Because Philip was a Greek name, meaning "lover of horses," these strangers had sought help from one they supposed was a fellow countryman. But suspicious of the interest of any Gentile in the Kingdom Crusade, Philip decided that he had better check with Andrew first—this disciple also having a Greek name, meaning "manly." But Andrew, ready as ever to share his faith, took full responsibility for bringing the Greeks to Jesus.

"So Philip informed Andrew and both went to tell Jesus." Moved by the hunger of these Gentiles for truth, Jesus opened his heart and talked to them about life and death, suffering and salvation. "He said to them, 'The hour has come for the Son of Man to be glorified. In solemn truth I tell you that unless a kernel of wheat falls into a furrow and dies, it remains a single kernel. But when it thus dies, it produces a whole head of wheat. The man who loves his own life will lose it, but he who yields up his life in this world will come safely into eternal life. Whoever serves me must follow me, for wherever I am shall my servant be. And my Father will honor whoever serves me'" (Jn.12:20-26).

John does not say, unfortunately, how the Greeks responded to the Good News; but whatever their response, with Andrew's help they had met the Master and had heard his call to discipleship. Not content to be a terminus for the revelation of God in Jesus, Andrew the Sharer sought instead to be a relay-station.

In his Beecher Lectures on Preaching, the author of "O Little Town of Bethlehem," Phillips Brooks, describes the effect that Jesus had on his disciples: "When his treatment of them was complete, they stood fused like glass, able to take God's truth in perfectly on one side and send it out perfectly on the other side of their transparent natures." Thus, real-life saints are remarkably similar to images in stained-glass windows, in that they are individuals through whom the glory of God shines, transmitting to others on their "manward side" the light received on their "Godward side."

Andrew knew how to do this, and in that way he is an example for us!

IV. Andrew The Neglected

In the earliest days of Jesus' ministry Andrew was a mem-

ber of the inner circle which was composed of Peter, James,
John and himself. For a time these four were all the disciples
Jesus had. But when opposition began to rear its ugly head
Jesus decided to enlarge his training class. He added eight
others, to round out the number to a symbolic Twelve. But
with this enlargement the inner circle became smaller;
Andrew was no longer included. From the fourth chapter of
Mark, his name appears only once, and that in conjunction
with the other three. His final mention in the New Testament
is in Acts 1:12 where, as in the Synoptic Gospels, he is simply
listed as one of the disciples. Peter, James and John are fea-
tured numbers of times, clearly in the spotlight, but Andrew
has disappeared. The three went with Jesus to Jairus' house,
leaving Andrew behind (Mk. 5:37). When Jesus went on a spiritual retreat (tradition tells us he went to Mount Hermon) and
was there transfigured, Andrew remained with the others (Mk.
9:2). And in his hour of crisis in Gethsemane, Jesus asked only
Peter, James and John to go further into the Garden with him.
The record does not tell us how Andrew may have felt. Here
was the very first of the disciples, for months a member of the
chosen few and a friendly person who sought to bring people
into the Kingdom Crusade, now slipping back into obscurity!
The Bible does not say outright that he did thus slip; it merely
permits him to. Why did this happen?

It might be that Andrew simply did not grow in his understanding of Jesus' mission as fast as the other three disciples.
Through some inherent inability to meet the qualifications
for holding cabinet rank, he moved back from the spotlighted
stage apron to backstage. If this were the case, however, it
would not have made him any less a model Christian. God
does not demand that we all reach the same lofty level of
leadership. All he demands is that we put to the best possible
use whatever loaves and fishes are ours to distribute. To deny
Andrew a place up stage is not to put him out of the theater.

For from what sparse evidence we have about Andrew's character, the moment that he found he was no longer to be in the footlights, he went quietly to work as one of the stagehands. He would have been in solid agreement with Dwight L. Moody when that evangelist exclaimed, "Don't go around mourning because you haven't someone else's gift. Take the armor that God has given you; and if he has given you a sling and a little stone, go out and do your work!"

It is also possible that Andrew, lacking the spectacular potential for spiritual growth which Simon Peter possessed, gradually found himself overshadowed by his impulsive brother. This may well explain why Mark's Gospel tells us so little about Andrew, for it is primarily Peter's own intensely personal reminiscence. And Matthew carried over this emphasis on Peter when he used perhaps as much as nine-tenths of Mark when writing his Gospel.

But one cannot believe that Andrew's being eclipsed by Peter or any other of the disciples really would have bothered him very much.

Helen Keller once said, in the same spirit, "I long to accomplish a great and noble task, but it is my chief duty and joy to accomplish humble tasks as though they were great and noble .... For the world is moved along, not only by the mighty shoves of its heroes, but also by the aggregate of tiny pushes of each honest worker." Commonsense wisdom from an amazing woman, whose accomplishment was far greater than she realized! The world's Simon Peters need the world's Andrews. If someone were to write a book entitled, "The Preaching Values of 'The Wizard of Oz,'" one chapter might well be devoted to how an 800-pound, opium-drugged lion was hauled out of a deadly poppy-field by thousands of field mice!

It is equally possible that Andrew might have been fully as worthy of standing in the spotlight as any other disciple, but was not as fortunate as the Big Three in his public relations. He lacked an admirer to whom he could dictate his memoirs. If we know little about him, it is not because he was not worth knowing but because nobody happened to preserve his words and deeds for posterity.

It is necessary to remember that the New Testament provides only factional information about the founding and growth of the Christian churches of the Middle East. There are great gaps which we shall never be able to fill except by conjecture or lucky archaeological finds. In fact, the "Acts of the Apostles" should have been entitled, "Some of the Acts of a Few of the Apostles," to emphasize how fragmentary is its record. We are not told, for example, how the church in Damascus, which received and nurtured the blinded Paul after his conversion, was founded. We know nothing about the origins of the church in Rome, which by the year 64 was big enough to survive the loss of large number of members in Nero's persecution. We are in almost complete ignorance about the seven churches of Asia Minor—Ephesus, Smyrna, Pergamum, Thyatira, Sardis, Philadelphia and Laodicea.

This means that an enormous amount of hard and dangerous missionary work was accomplished by a great many men and women who were even less fortunate than Andrew in their public relations. There are scores of names listed in the New Testament such as Prochorus and Nicanor, Timon and Parmenas, Nicolaus and Rhoda, Lucius of Cyrene, Dionysius the Areopagite, Manaen and Damaris, Crispus, and others whose names mean nothing to us today because there is no information about them. Converts like these worked behind the scenes, away from the spotlights. Their names are known to us but their work is known only to God. Yet without their labors the church could not have survived.

And consider how many more faithful souls are never even mentioned in the New Testament! There must even be

numbers whose names, are not known to us because no records exist of their accomplishments. Indeed, we can deduce
their existence only because certain areas of the Middle East
which were at one time known to be pagan were suddenly
discovered to be Christian, with no evidence as to how their
conversion had taken place. Certainly an angel did not wave a
magic wand and effect the change. Such evangelization occurred only because unknown disciples preached and lived
the way of Christ. It may be that for every follower of Jesus
who is named in the New Testament, there were a thousand
other followers who behind the scenes "fought the good fight,
finished the race, kept the faith," and for whom was "laid up
the crown of righteousness" (2Tim.4:7,8 RSV).

Andrew the Neglected is the patron saint of this vast company of unknown disciples. But tradition gives him a wider
"sainthood" than this.

V. Andrew the Thrice-Sainted

In his final appearance to the Eleven, Jesus gave this instruction: "Go and make disciples of everyone in the world,
baptizing them in the name of the Father, and the Son, and of
the Holy Spirit, teaching them to obey all my commandments. And I will be with you always, to the very end of time"
(Mt.28:19,20). The first historian of the early church, Eusebius,
states that when each disciple was allotted an area, Andrew
drew a tough assignment. He was to go to Scythia, a territory
bounded by the Black Sea and the Danube and Tanis rivers,
which was occupied by a fierce barbaric tribe with an awe-
some reputation for cruelty. It is a wonder that he survived.
Because this area was part of Russia, Andrew has become a
patron saint of the Russian people.

"The Acts of Andrew," written perhaps two hundred years
after the apostle's death, states that he later moved south into
the part of Greece known by its Roman name, Provincia

Achaia. There Andrew found a situation which at first seemed favorable for effective testimony about Jesus. Maximilla, the wife of the Roman governor Aegeas, was lying at death's door, and Aegeas had sworn to kill himself when she died. Andrew healed her, and for a time must have enjoyed high favor. He also cured the servant of the governor's brother, Stratocles. Trouble began, however, when Maximilla, Stratocles and his servant became Christians. A main theme of this "Acts of Andrew" is that Christian women married to pagan husbands should get a divorce in order to achieve perfect santification. If Andrew had thus advised Maximilla, this could have been the cause for his arrest. He was sentenced to die as his Master had died, on a cross. First he was beaten with rods and then tied, not nailed, to an X-shaped cross, so that he would perish slowly from exposure. This tradition states that it took three days for him to die, but that he kept telling people about Jesus till the end. His martyrdom occurred in the city of Patras, a port on the Gulf of Corinth in the year 69, on the thirtieth of November, today observed as Saint Andrew's Day. That Sunday closest to his Day is the First Sunday in Advent. Today he is also one of the patron saints of Greece.

In the year 313 the Roman emperor Flavius Valerius Constantinus (Constantine) proclaimed the Edict of Milan which made Christianity legal throughout the Empire. Although not baptized till he was dying, he was cordial to the Faith, probably due to the influence of his Christian mother, Helena. He moved the capital from Rome to Byzantium, which he renamed Constantinople (now Istanbul), and in 330 dedicated it as a Christian city. No pagan shrines or heathen buildings were permitted.

In order to make his new city more worthy of being the world's Christian capital, Constantine the Great began to make collections of early Christiana. His mother went to Palestine, officially located some of the historic sites of the new faith including the Holy Sepulchre, and came back not only with loads of artifacts, but also with the "true cross." To her findings he added many of his own.

In his autobiography, *The Harvest of the Years*, Rockwell Harmon Potter, one-time Dean of Hartford Theological Seminary, tells about an elderly New England farmer who became envious of neighbors who were busily collecting this and that, while he had no collection at all. One day through a sudden inspiration he made out genealogical tables and launched a search for the last resting-places of his ancestors. When he would locate a grandfather in an obscure burying ground in another township he would write for permission to remove the body to his new private cemetery off in the "back forty." The selectmen invariably would reply, "Yes, so long as it don't run to money!" He persisted in garnering his ancestors till his "collection" of over thirty bodies was complete for four generations back, and he had become the talk of several townships!

Constantine had a similar interest. He learned in 337 that the remains of St. Andrew were buried at Patras, within the boundaries of the Empire. Immediately he ordered the coffin to be exhumed and brought to Constantinople — a more fitting place for the Protokletos to lie.

But some four hundred years later a monk named Regulus had a vision in which an angel commanded him to remove part of the saint's remains — specifically, a tooth, an armbone, a kneecap and three fingerbones from the right hand, identifiable parts which had not returned to dust — and head westward. As he traveled up the English Channel his ship was driven by a storm to the coast of Scotland. Taking this as a sign that his journey was over, he disembarked, built a church whose ruins still stand, named the parish St. Andrew and established himself as its initial bishop. (The world's first golf course was created in "S'Nandrews," although there appears to be no historical connection between the two events!)

This saga of the apostle's relics was not too unusual, for bones had a way of rising and traveling in those days. For example, there is a similar tradition that states that after Pontius Pilate's death in Rome, having been recalled from Judea in disgrace, his body was tossed into the Tiber River. But the river roiled in such anger at being polluted by one who had betrayed the Son of God equally as much as Judas, that it was removed and thrown into the Rhone River. After it had been summarily rejected there, also, it was carted to Vienne, the presumed place of Pilate's exile, now in France. There it was sunk in a small lake on Mount Pilatus which is southwest of Lake Lucerne. Being too small to follow the outraged example of the big rivers, the little lake still shows its indignation by kicking up unexpectedly severe storms! But one may move serenely to the crest of the 7,000-foot mountain named for Pilate by cable car.

Bones alone, however, do not turn an apostle into a patron saint. This happened to Andrew only after his relics exerted influence on Scottish history. According to an ancient legend, the Scots were about to attack an invading English army, and during the night St. Andrew appeared in a vision to the King of the Picts, saying that on the morrow he would defeat the invaders. The next morning as the Picts advanced shouting "St. Andrew, our Patron Saint, be our guide!" a fiery X-shaped cross appeared in the sky. Terrified, the English fled in utter rout. The historic flag of Scotland keeps this legend alive, and the white cross on a sky-blue background became a part of the Union Jack when England and Scotland were united under James I.

Andrew the First-Called! Andrew the Persuader! Andrew the Sharer! Andrew the Thrice-Sainted! Andrew the Neglected, the symbol of the unnoticed, the unhonored, the overlooked! Andrew, the Patron Saint of the vast company of Unknown Disciples! Though first among the followers of Jesus, he was content to become the last. His brother became the greatest of the disciples, but he found no shame in being one of the least. Denied stardom, he joined those whose quiet labors made stardom possible for others.

Marking the grave of a rugby player at one of the colleges in Oxford, there is a tombstone which bears this high tribute: "He played four years on the scrubs." He never got out of the minor leagues, but he kept right on playing, just like Andrew.

It might be Andrew, too, who speaks to us through these lines of B. Y. Williams:

"O Master, I would play the violin.
Pray try me, I am really not unskilled."
The Master with a patient gesture stilled
The ardent voice. "The music must begin.
Seest thou for violins I have no need.
Back to the woodwinds: take thine own bassoon
And play thy part." The strings were all in tune,
The brasses ready. Still the voice did plead:
"O Master, I play only three short bars."
"Thou playest the bassoon well. No more entreat.
Thy three short bars are needed to complete
The music that shall lift men to the stars."
O soul, play well the few notes given thee:
The Master needs them for life's symphony.

In a real sense, then, is not Andrew the patron saint of ordinary pew-sitters! Does not everyone within the Christian enterprise today need just this sort of reassurance—that although the spotlight may rarely, if ever, play on us, yet what we are and what we do for God and our fellows are known and treasured by the Almighty, and that our names are written in his Book of Life!

Chapter Four

The Brothers Tumultuous

ONE of the most colorful individuals in major league baseball was the author of the book, *Nice Guys Finish Last!* His temper was so delicately balanced that it teetered up and down in a light breeze; and to it was attached his tongue. The moment a cloud of any size appeared, it was whipped up into a storm. Early in his career a nickname was hung on him by someone who enjoyed watching his famous harangues — one which stuck to him unshakably because it encapsulated his most dominant characteristic: "Leo the Lip" Durocher.

Some fan, player, umpire or sportswriter gave Mr. Durocher his nickname. History conferred on Thomas the undeserved sobriquet, "The Doubter." But James and John, like Peter, received theirs directly from an unimpeachable source, Jesus himself. And unlike Peter's it was not complimentary. For when listing the disciples, Mark states, "He appointed twelve to be with him, and to be sent out to preach and have authority to cast out demons: Simon, whom he surnamed Peter; James the son of Zebedee and John the brother of James, whom he surnamed Boanerges, that is, sons of thunder" (Mk.3:14-17 RSV).

122

The Aramaic equivalent of this Greek term, however, is stronger than in Mark's translation, and should read, "sons of tumult!" We learn more from this detail as to what they were really like than from clues about family background.

Their mother, Salome, may have been a sister of Mary; if so, they were cousins of Jesus. The presence of hired men suggests that their family income was better than average. James was the elder, since he is mentioned first. With Peter the two brothers constituted an intimate inner core of support on which Jesus relied at key times in his ministry — especially at the transfiguration (Mk.9:2-8) and in Gethsemane (Mk.14:32f.). For when Jesus named them "Boanerges" the English equivalent would be something like "Big-mouth James" and "John the Bombastic." Apparently men of low boiling-point and ready indignation, they were not averse to "shooting off their mouths" before taking careful aim. Habitually they sounded off aggressively against whatever displeased them. They were always "where the action is" because much of the time, unfortunately, they created it. They call to mind one of Paul Bunyan's friends, Guns Gunderson, who was known as "Shot Gunderson" because of his explosive temper!

Although such judgments about the characters of these brothers sound harsh, they are verified by the Gospel accounts. The disciples appear to have been paired off, and in each of the three recorded instances in which James and John worked together, they became the center of an unhappy commotion which fully justified Jesus' calling them the Thunderers.

I. Petty Officiousness

The earliest incident is related by Mark. "One day John came to Jesus and exclaimed excitedly, 'Master, we caught a fellow casting out evil spirits in your name, and we warned

him to stop because he isn't one of us'" (Mk.9:38). The bare
bones of this sentence may be fleshed out in some such
fashion as this: James and John had been away from the main
band of disciples on an errand in a neighboring village, when
they were attracted by a crowd of people in the public square.
Accustomed to being at the center of crowds in places of
honor as disciples of the Master who taught and healed with
divine authority, and not as spectators out on the periphery,
they elbowed their way to the middle to learn what was going
on. Their attention was caught by a cluster of three persons,
the two nearer men restraining by force a teen-age youth who
groaned, tossed his head wildly, ground his teeth and twisted
to escape.

"Why, the boy is possessed by a demon!" thought John. "I
wonder whether I dare use my authority here?" Even as this
thought took shape he noted opposite the three a man whom
he instantly identified as a familiar type of itinerant preacher
such as occasionally appeared in Capernaum and Bethsaida.
John had never seen the man before, and intuitively sensed
that he was witnessing the beginning of competition in an
area where Jesus thus far had enjoyed a monopoly—the
healing arts. John grudgingly admitted that the light of compassion was in the preacher's eyes as he laid gnarled hands
gently on the sick youth's head. But the disciple was startled
and then angered when the preacher said in a loud voice to
the sufferer, "O evil spirit, come out of this lad. I command
you in the name of Jesus of Nazareth!"

The youth gave a sudden convulsive leap and then sagged
limply to the ground. His relatives stretched him out on the
cobblestones and one of them knelt at his side. Then looking
up fearfully he exclaimed, "He's dead!"

The preacher shook his head. "He is sleeping," he said
calmly. "When he awakes he will be in his right mind. The
demon is gone, thanks to the power of Jesus of Nazareth."

At these words the tongue of John the Bombastic came unstuck. With a bellow of rage he pushed forward to confront the astonished healer. Here was not even honest competition, but fraudulent imitation! The man was operating in the Master's name without a license!

"By what right do you use the name of Jesus?" he thundered. His voice carried far out over the crowd and quelled the rising exclamations of wonder at the cure. "Did our Master authorize you to do this sort of thing, as he did me? Of course not, and don't try to tell me that he did. I'm one of his chief disciples, a member of his inner circle, and I've never laid eyes on you before. You've absolutely no right to steal our act, and I command you to stop!"

Still "breathing out threatenings and slaughter," John turned to leave, with James close behind. As he plowed through the lane which silently opened for him, he thundered back over his shoulder, "You can be sure that Jesus will learn at once what has been going on behind his back!"

As John strode off, muttering incoherently, James may have said to him doubtfully, "I know how you feel, but after all, the lad was healed."

"Ha! For how long?" his brother snorted. "Besides, no one has a right to use the Master's name and power without specific permission. Do you want Galilee overrun with shoddy imitators? Look at what that would do to our Kingdom Crusade. Think how it would affect our own influence."

Thus on reaching Jesus, John exclaimed, "Master, there's some dirty work going on that you ought to know about." He paused dramatically, savoring in advance the shock that his news would bring.

Jesus sighed. "What is it this time, O Thunderer?"

Something in Jesus' manner curbed John's belligerency. "When you called us," he began more quietly, "you gave us authority to cast out demons, but not to anyone else. Remember? Well, over in that village there we encountered a hobo preacher who was casting out demons in your name!" And as the memory of his irritation returned, he cried indignantly, "Think of that Master! The gall of him! James and I commanded him to stop because he is not part of our Kingdom Crusade."

Here the brothers gave evidence that highhandedly *they* had assumed the right to make edicts in Jesus' name. They further demonstrated that they regarded the Kingdom Crusade as the new, divinely-appointed religious Establishment which had superseded the old establishment which was no longer in God's favor.

True enough, Jesus and his disciples had learned the hard way that the Jerusalem hierarchy was their chief enemy. Any Establishment has a way of ultimately betraying the causes it was created to defend. A case in point is the Bible passage quoted by Jesus when he cleansed the temple: "Does not Scripture state, 'My house shall be known as a house of prayer for all the nations?'" The words are God's, spoken through Isaiah's prophecy that Israel is called to offer to all mankind the spiritual insights which God has entrusted to her (Is.56:7). Yet the Establishment of Jesus' day had posted a sign in the Jerusalem temple warning Gentiles not to enter the Court of Israel:

LET NO ALIEN ENTER
WITHIN THE BALUSTRADE AND EMBANKMENT
ABOUT THE SANCTUARY.
WHOEVER IS CAUGHT
MAKES HIMSELF RESPONSIBLE FOR HIS DEATH
WHICH WILL FOLLOW.

What a welcome to possible converts! Here is demonstrated the age-old truth that every needed reform, such as Jesus', must run the gauntlet of the Establishment's entrenched and unscrupulous power.

Thus Jesus had every reason to distrust the very idea of Establishments. Yet, here all of a sudden, he discovered that two of his disciples had formed a Counter-Establishment and were already enforcing certain membership rules!

There must be rules and regulations to govern enterprises, of course, such as the announcement before a televised baseball game:

"This telecast comes to you by the authority of major league baseball and is intended solely for your private, non-commercial use. Any publication, re-transmission or other use of these descriptions and accounts without the express written consent of the Commissioner of Baseball, is strictly prohibited."

Here is a legitimate use of authority by the baseball Establishment. Such authority must exist or chaos would ensue. Otherwise a manager might declare arbitrarily that he was free to enter a player twice in a game; a player thumbed out of the game might refuse to go; or an umpire might state that three balls now consitute a walk.

But had not James and John made an illegitimate use of their authority? Had they not decreed, without authorization from Jesus, that no one outside their little messianic Establishment might emulate Jesus without explicit permission from one of them? Here was arrogance in the name of religion; that type of arrogance is still with us today.

Years ago on a camping trip we came late one afternoon to a small South Dakota town. Friendly little signs had directed us to an area reserved for overnight camping. While the boys were unloading the tents a small boy appeared and marched up to me. Tilting his head far back so that he could look at me down his nose, he said officiously, "My father is the mayor. You can't camp here unless he says so." Unspoken was another sentence, "And I am his deputy!"

Amused, I said, "Come along." Taking his reluctant hand, I

led him to a freshly-painted sign. "Read it. He has already given us permission."

The boy read the lettering to himself, his mouth shaping the words:

> OVERNIGHT CAMPING WELCOMED
> PLEASE SIGN THE GUEST REGISTER
> PLEASE KEEP THE GROUNDS CLEAN

He looked at me down his nose again, not one bit fazed. "All right," he said with a lordly wave of his hand, "you can stay. But don't throw any garbage around." With that he turned and marched off, a miniature lordling in a miniature Establishment which his father did not dream was in existence. Although the religious aspect was missing, here was a future James or John come to life in the twentieth century.

What was Jesus' reaction to John's report about attempting to silence competition? Undoubtedly he sighed as he said to the brothers, "You did wrong to forbid him. And you have no right to make edicts of your own." Thinking of the enemies who were already multiplying about him, very likely he added, "Do we not need all the friends we can find? Does not God welcome anyone who does good in my name? Remember, O Thunderers, that he who is not against us is for us!"

It may be, also, that John remonstrated with Jesus. "Now, hold on, Master!" he may have cried. "That preacher didn't belong to our Crusade. Are you going to let your power be mishandled by any old person who comes along?"

Then Jesus, drawing on the special store of patience he reserved particularly for use with his disciples, may well have replied, "John, the Good News is not copyrighted. Everyone can have it without paying any licensing fee. It belongs in the public domain. There is no room for exclusivism in faith. The only requirements in the use of my name or my revelation of God are sincerity and inclusiveness. When anyone uses my name with integrity and generousness of spirit, God hears and answers his prayer."

Yet in spite of Jesus' unequivocal attitude, do not many modern disciples pollute practices of their faith with a four-fold exclusivism which states in effect, "Birds of a feather should flock together!"

There is a racially-prejudiced exclusivism which declares, "White churches for whites only!" Blacks are free to remain in their own religious institutions! Racially-inclusive churches are still in a minority today, because most white Americans still want to belong to a lily-white congregation.

Years ago when rumor spread that a black family was considering uniting with a church I was serving, the patriarch of an influential clan within our membership came to my study. "The minute that family moves in," he thundered, "we all will move out."

"That sounds like a threat," I said.

"No," he grated. "It's a promise."

Events later proved that the black family was committed to a friendlier congregation, so that our congregation was stuck with that "apostle of exclusivism" and his clan. One of the most grievous of sins is the spiritual arrogance which results when whites who think that they are within the inner circle of disciples — like James and John — deny similar stature to blacks or anyone else.

There is a class-conscious exclusivism which restricts membership according to the requirements of wealth, ancestry or social position. Since 1930 I have been associated with almost every kind of church — western home missionary and urban wealthy, New England mill village and metropolitan suburban, urban "problem" area and coastal summer colony. Yet I have never known a church which did not contain some form of class snobbery. Milkman Jones, for example, who works for H. Pauncefort Langeworthy's Sunshine Dairy would certainly never be turned away from the sculptured outer doors of his boss' swank church. But because he does not "belong" in the inner circle with James and John, interior doors of warm fellowship are not willingly opened to him. Certain individuals have said privately, "Well, Tom Jones is not quite the caliber we would like for a Minute-Man; he would be happier in the Men's Club." And others have said, "Unfortunately, Jane Jones is not just the right material for our Study Group. Maybe the Quilters would like to have her." Thus, instead of feeling that they are in a cordial company of disciples, Tom and Jane have the sensation of standing alone in a dark corridor of a strange hotel, with people going in and out of doors where they may not follow. Such selfish isolation hurts the Langeworthys equally as much as the Joneses, and makes a mockery of Christian fellowship.

There is an exclusivism based on intellectual pride. There are churches whose leading members are so proud of their collective educational attainments—"We have twenty-four Ph.D's. on our active roll!"—and so awed by the massive erudition of their minister, the Reverend Doctor James John Boanerges, that they wish to be known as "The Thinking Man's Church." "None of this treacherous, ephemeral emotionalism, you know!" Such persons privately resent those within the membership who are merely "domesticated fowl" content to scratch in the barnyard dust; but they eagerly welcome the "eagles" who are able to climb sunward with them into the intellectual heights. Yet is an exclusive circle of burgeoning brains any more Christlike than one of bulging billfolds or an all-white décor?

There is also the exclusivism produced by one demonination's sense of superiority over another. Sectarian pride—usually based on the shakiest of foundations—sometimes betrays modern disciples into shocking forms of religious prejudice. A man once said to me, "That fellow doesn't know the first thing about authentic Christianity. You see, he attends Immaculate Conception Church." This may be interpreted to mean, "He's just out of it. He's not one of us." Recently within my hearing a woman said to her bus seat-mate, "Of course she won't be a good neighbor. She's joined the Jehovah's Witnesses!" This may be interpreted to mean, "Neighborliness is limited to us Baptists and Presbyterians!" In describing the United Church of Christ to a Southern Baptist who had never heard of it, a minister said, "Well, it is sort of the educated branch of the Baptist Church!" This may be interpreted as an attempt at humor gone awry. An evangelist once concluded a bitter disagreement with another churchman with these biting words: "Very well, you go on in your way, and I'll go on in God's!" This needs no interpretation.

Thus in such fashions as these many persons include themselves and their bosom companions in some select inner circle which, encased in an ecclesiastical edifice and buttressed with pious covenants, they mistakenly call a church. But is not this attitude identical to James' and John's when they faced the itinerant preacher? Their spiritual arrogance had to be knocked out of them before James would be a worthy enough disciple to be martyred, and before John could be known one day as "the Beloved Disciple."

And is not the same true of us, as well? Theological convictions are necessary and important, of course. But as long as we draw any kind of biblically unjustified restrictive lines in Jesus' name, we are exclaiming with John, "Master, they don't belong to us. They aren't our kind!" The only escape from the sin of exclusivism is to stop creating inner circles for the private purpose of (in Sam Goldwyn's picturesque phrase) "including someone out," and to begin creating larger fellowships for overcoming whatever illegitimate divisiveness now exists. For when we come to sense Jesus' remarkable consciousness of human solidarity, we will draw the entire membership in Jesus' name into one worshiping community. Then the unChristlike hunger for belonging to some inner circle, with its proud privilege of preferential fellowship with Peter, James and John, will vanish from all hearts and minds.

II. Hunger for Vengeance

A second occasion for thundering is related in Luke's Gospel. "As the time drew near for Jesus to be sacrificed, he firmly made up his mind to go to Jerusalem. He sent messengers ahead to a Samaritan village to make arrangements for their coming, but the villagers would not entertain them because they knew he was going to Jerusalem. When James and John reported this, they said, 'Master, let's call down fire from heaven and burn them up, as Elijah did!'" (Lk.9:51-54).

A brief excursion into Old Testament history enlarges our understanding of this fire-and-brimstone suggestion. When Ahaziah, King of Israel, was severely injured by a fall from his bedroom window, he sent messengers to the priests of Baalzebub, the god of Ekron, to inquire if his injury was fatal. We learn in the first chapter of II Kings that the prophet Elijah met the messengers at a strategic spot along the road and said sternly, "Is it because Israel no longer has any God that you must be sent to consult a false god in another country? You cannot learn the truth of the king's condition in Ekron. Go back to Samaria and say to Ahaziah, 'Thus saith the Lord: "You shall never leave the bed on which you are lying, and shall surely die."'"

When the king heard this dire pronouncement he exclaimed angrily, "I've had enough of Elijah, that troubler of Israel. Captain, take fifty men, arrest Elijah and bring him to me."

At first thought one wonders why so large a contingent was sent to apprehend one unarmed prophet. But Elijah's reputation was such that prudence was required. Ahaziah had not been prudent enough, however, for when the captain came to Elijah and said, "O man of God, you are under arrest," the prophet chanted toward the sky, "Let fire come down from heaven and consume these men." And it did.

In greater rage the king sent another captain with fifty men, who suffered a like fate. When the third detachment arrived, in great dread of annihilation, and praying for its life, Elijah finally consented to go to the palace because he knew that the king now dared not harm him.

This ancient story about the prophet became part of the common knowledge of every Israelite. About nine hundred years after Elijah's death, James and John were reminded of it because of what they felt to be parallel circumstances. Besides, they may also have based their request on a much more recent precedent. For when Jesus sent his disciples out on their first field trip he said to them, "When anyone or any village refuses to entertain you or listen to your message, shake its dust from your shoes as you leave. For I tell you that Sodom and Gomorrah suffered an easier fate than will that village" (Mt.10:14,15). Now Sodom and Gomorrah had been destroyed by fire from heaven, so was not Jesus approving such punishment for villages which rejected him?

Another indication of the brothers' hunger for vengeance occurs when Jesus made up his mind to carry the Kingdom Crusade to the fountainhead of his nation's life, the capital city. He was up in the former northern kingdom of Israel, and in order to reach Jerusalem, which was within the old southern kingdom of Judah, he had to pass through Samaria — an east-west corridor, dating from the Babylonian Captivity, that separated these territories. Samaria was inhabited largely by non-Jewish persons who practiced a form of Judaism which the Jews detested as a poor imitation. Bad feelings had existed for centuries between the Samaritans and their neighbors, and frequently the people of Samaria made trouble for those who traveled between Judah and Israel.

Upon reaching the border of Samaria, Jesus sent James

and John ahead to arrange for overnight accommodations. When the band arrived at the chosen village toward sundown, footsore, dusty, tired, ready for hot food, a cooling footbath and a comfortable bed, the brothers met them at the outskirts and warned them away. Some recent run-in with other Jewish travelers had aroused the village to such an extent that they were driving Jews away. Innocent of troublemaking though Jesus and his party were, they suffered as the innocent always suffer from the sins and prejudices of others. A modern parallel is the fact that if a tourist's passport reveals that he has come directly from Israel, he will not be admitted to an Arab country.

Thus James and John, who had borne the brunt of the enmity, were angry clean through. One of them burst out, "Why, Master, this is intolerable! Who do those Samaritans think they are, slamming their doors in our faces! Why, you are the Christ, God's Son. They can't do this to you!"

And the other, remembering how Elijah had handled a similar threat to his prophetic status — and how his response apparently had Jesus' approval — exclaimed vehemently, "Lord, do you want us to call down fire from heaven, as Elijah did, and destroy this whole rotten village? Just say the word and we'll do it. You bet we'll do it!" Was not the offense considerably more serious this time because One greater than Elijah was with them.

The record indicates that they really thought they had the power to wreak Sodom's destruction on the Samaritans. They actually believed God would respond to their command with complete annihilation. Similarly, there are Sons of Tumult today who believe that if enough Christians would pray hard enough, God would wipe the Soviet Union out of existence! James and John certainly knew that Samaritans always acted unpredictably; but when a simple request for traditional Mid east hospitality was thrown back in their faces, their anger took the form of a vindictive desire to avenge the insult by a Hiroshima-like holocaust. Theirs was the narrow nationalistic view of a Jonah who would rather have had the city of Nineveh destroyed than redeemed by the love of God. They put their mouths where their common sense ought to have been.

Mark Twain once described a steamboat whose boiler was so small and whose steam whistle was so large that whenever the captain pulled the whistle cord the paddle wheels stopped. This may be an analogy of the way in which the sons of Zebedee met any crisis — thundering instead of thinking. With some individuals,

> When the mouth flies open with chatter
>   The ears go shut with a snap,
> The mind withdraws from such clatter,
>   And the soul lies down for a nap.

This may have been true for James and John. True enough, they had been living for many months in intimate fellowship with Jesus. They had seen how the Master's compassion had reached out toward persons regardless of how good or bad they were. They had listened while Jesus talked to the crowds about the Kingdom of God, in which they might live here and now. They had received, at odd moments during the day, additional instruction as to how a citizen of that new Kingdom should behave. They had steadily been immersed in the Christian ideal since the day they were called — and yet how little of it appears to have soaked in! How contemporary with us they are! They had failed to understand that Jesus brought a fresh revelation of God's will for mankind which completed the work of the Prophets. Previous ideas and attitudes had become outmoded by the Good News. The most striking aspect of this New Covenant, which Jeremiah had foreseen as one day replacing the Law of Moses (31:31f.), was the elevating of the personal relation between individuals and their fellows. It was to be a relationship of love compounded of three special ingredients:

    1) Outgoing affection which does not ask, "Is he worth loving?" or "What's in it for me?";

    2) Dynamic concern that the individual shall realize his God-given potential in character and personality; and

    3) Boundless goodwill for every person, no matter how that person may act in return.

Vengeance for wrongs, as James and John were proposing, has no place in Christlike behavior.

Years ago at a religious convocation at Grinnell College in Iowa, the question "What is the Christian attitude toward the Negro?" was being discussed. An elderly man arose and said, "I have lived for many years in Atlanta, and have been in continuing relation with Negroes. And I have learned that I can love them even though I rarely like them."

Immediately the hall was in an uproar as person after person jumped up to ridicule or excoriate what was said. Of course, the color of a person's skin is irrelevant. But I have always felt a keen sense of indebtedness to that unknown man for showing me in a flash the essence of Christian love — the ability to offer outgoing affection, dynamic concern and boundless willing of good to those whom I do not like, as much as to those whom I do like.

This teaching of Jesus was so radical for his day that it usually fell on uncomprehending ears. Indeed, it was so far removed from their usual habits of thought and conduct that James and John did not take Jesus' teaching seriously. To them the inhospitable prejudice of the Samaritans was a grievous affront. They reacted not in accordance with the new commandment of love, but with the Old Testament habit of retributive justice. Just as though Jesus, and before him the prophets, had never lived, the Thunderers reverted to the murderous practice attributed to Elijah, which makes the punishment far heavier than the crime. Indeed, they went all the way back to the fiercely primitive days of Lamech and his song of vindictive vengeance:

Adah and Zillah, hear my voice,
  you wives of Lamech, hearken to what I say:
I have slain a man for wounding me,
  a young man for bruising me:
If Cain is avenged sevenfold,
  truly Lamech seventy and sevenfold.

(Gn.4:23,24 RSV)

How did Jesus feel when the brothers eagerly asked not just to get even with the Samaritans but to obliterate them? He had worked especially hard with Peter, James and John, and yet after many months could see little change in them. He had taught them that when someone offended them, they were to invert Lamech's revenge and forgive seventy times seven times. A forgiving spirit does not keep books. Forgiveness is not a medicine to be prescribed only on particular occasions; rather, it is a continuing attitude applicable equally to every personal relationship. Jesus had shown them all this, and still the brothers acted big-mouthed and bombastic toward that village.

We get no clue from Luke as to Jesus' reaction to the bloodthirsty request of the two brothers. The record states simply that Jesus "turned and reproved them sharply; and they went on to another village" (Lk.9:55,56). As is so often the case, the record leaves to our imagination Jesus' disappointment and despair over his disciples' lack of spiritual perceptivity. Other ancient manuscripts state that he added, "You are forgetting your spiritual nature, for the Son of Man did not come to destroy men's lives, but to save them."

But we today must not be too hard on James and John.

For in our own personal relationships how much better than they do we follow the law of love? How easy is it for us to reply to a personal insult with sincere affection? How recently have we expressed Christlike concern for a trouble-making neighbor with whom we cannot get along? How long has it been since we have felt any surge of goodwill for the people of the Soviet Union, China or Cuba? Is not the principle that love is the law of life just as radical and unrealistic for us now after 2,000 years of exposure to it, as it was for the Bombastic Brothers who had heard it for the first time? How often is forgiveness regarded, instead, as being a pious idea which is not practicable in any emergency!

Back in my home missionary days on the Western plains, certain members of our little church became incensed at a "Single Gospel" group which insisted on using our church building while at the same time causing us as much trouble as it could. Many of our members demanded that we lock them out of the building, and give them a taste of their own meanness. I replied that we should set them an example in Christlike behavior, and permit them to continue using our building. One cattleman said, "Now, Reverend, you know as well as I do that this other church has smashed everything to pieces in our village. They don't deserve the kindness you aim to give 'em. I say it's dangerous to do it. It's like pitchin' camp in a rattler's den."

Another joined the discussion. "Look, Reverend," he said irritably, "when you find a tick on you, you burn him off quick as you can. That's what we should do with them Single Gospelers."

Clem Murdock, a sheepman, likewise added his objections. "Tell me, just what do you think is gonna happen from treating those Gospelers so nice? Are they gonna come around like flop-eared hounds to lick your hand? Are they gonna quit peddling lies about us—like that one about us being the servants of Antichrist? Huh! They'll take all the cuddling we give 'em, but you can bet your last quid of tobacco that they won't give us none back!"

"But Mr. Murdock," I said, "isn't it true that we can win only by being better Christians than they are, different from them? If we keep doing back to them everything they do to us, we'll become like them. Nobody in Beechmont or Prairieville will be able to see any difference between either church!"

But Clem turned away disgustedly. "Oh, you preachers are all alike," he snorted, "always talking about goodness and mercy right while somebody's cutting off your suspender buttons. I wonder why religion always makes a fellow softheaded."

Is not this interchange a modern expression of the age-old conflict between thirst for retributive justice and the command of Jesus? Is forgiveness actually an effective solvent for the hate-clotted relations between human beings? Or are those who practice it softheaded sentimentalists who make troubles worse with their impracticable ideals? The biblical record indicates that James and John began by feeling as Clem Murdock did — they rejected forgiveness and demanded revenge. And when Jesus would not consent to fire-bombing the Samaritans, their resentment must have smoldered for a time in some rear section of their emotions.

But just as Peter was finally changed from a sandlike to a rocklike disciple, so also the Thundering Brothers grew out of vindictiveness toward the Samaritans and came to show concern and good will! The eighth chapter of Acts reveals this heartening sequel.

When the newly-appointed deacon, Stephen, was stoned and became the first Christian martyr, the infant church was subjected to heavy persecution. Converts fled for their lives in all directions. One of the other deacons, whose name was Philip, "went down to a city of Samaria, and proclaimed to them the Christ. And the multitudes with one accord gave heed to what was said by Philip, for unclean spirits came out of many who were possessed, and many who were paralyzed or lame were healed. So there was much joy in that city" (Ac.8:5-8 RSV). The hated Samaritans were joining the Kingdom Crusade.

The record continues that "when the apostles at Jerusalem heard that Samaria had received the word of God, they sent to them Peter and John, who came down and prayed for them that they might receive the Holy Spirit; for he had not yet fallen on any of them, but they had only been baptized in the name of the Lord Jesus. Then they laid their hands on them, and they received the Holy Spirit.... Now when they (Peter and John) had testified and spoken the word of the Lord, they returned to Jerusalem, preaching the gospel to many villages of the Samaritans" (Ac.8:14-17,25 RSV). One can sense John's emotions as he came to that particular community which, years earlier, he had wanted to destroy!

What a dramatic change in John's bombastic attitude! When once he would have laid vengeful hands on them in wrath, now he laid praying hands on them in love. When once he would have called down withering fire to incinerate their bodies, now he called down the flame of the Holy Spirit to burn within their hearts. This is one reason why he became known as the "Beloved Disciple."

III. Request for Special Privilege

Just a few days after Jesus had rebuked the disciples for trying to establish a pecking order in the Kingdom Cause, the big-mouthed brothers again elbowed their way into the limelight. This time they had succumbed to the "Courtier Temptation," which causes ambitious individuals to use secret influence to rise higher on the ladder of success than their own talents would take them. Presuming on the fact that they were Jesus' cousins and might be considered to have "blood rights," they came to him privately with a selfish request. Matthew's account takes some of the onus of the incident from James' and John's shoulders and puts it on their mother's, stating that she was the one who engineered the incident. One can imagine, however, that crowding right up behind her, eagerly awaiting Jesus' reply, were her agressive sons.

Mark's account reads: "Master, we'd like you to say 'Yes' to something we want very badly."

If Jesus had been a parent, alarm-bells would certainly have begun ringing in his head. They probably did anyway, for he answered, "Just what is it you want me to do?"

"They said, 'Well, promise that when you come into your glory, one of us may sit at your right hand and the other at your left.'"

Assuming that Jesus would be president in the new order, they coveted for themselves the cabinet positions of vice-president and secretary of state.

This time Jesus did not rebuke them for their presumptuousness, because this was a matter of utmost gravity. He gave them a sober answer calculated to shake them into an awareness that they might be sharing not his glory but his agony.

"'You do not realize what you are asking,' he said. 'Are you willing to drink the cup which I drink? Are you ready to be baptized in the same fashion as I will be?'"

Not realizing that Jesus was speaking of possible arrest and execution, they shrugged off the warning and replied, "Sure, we're willing!"

"Jesus anered, 'You will indeed drink of the cup from which I drink and share the baptism which I undergo. But it is not my right to put just anyone either at my right hand or my left. Such places are reserved for those who deserve them the most'" (Mk.10:35-40).

Two things are contained in Jesus' reply. First, here was a

forecast of Jesus' coming martyrdom and the persecution
which all the disciples would share. Here was a foreshadowing of the troubles which inevitably beset the disciple in any
generation who seriously attempts to follow his Lord.

When Sir Ernest Shakelton sought personnel in 1900 for
his polar expedition, he ran this advertisement in the *London
Times*: "Men wanted for hazardous journey. Small wages, bitter cold, long months of complete darkness, constant danger,
safe return doubtful. Honor and recognition in case of success."

Similarly, Jesus did not invite his followers to any picnic,
saying, "Pick up a sandwich and come along!" Rather he said,
"Whoever would be my disciple must give up all claim to self
and follow me, accepting whatever cross may result. For the
one who hoards his life will impoverish it, whereas the one
who freely spends his life on my behalf will enrich it"
(Mt.16:24,25).

Second, in Jesus' reply to the brothers' request for top
rank in the new Kingdom is also found a blunt statement
about heaven's admissions policy: one cannot bargain or
bribe his way into immortality. Rather, it is a gift offered not
because of whatever earthly influence a person can summon
on his behalf, but because of what he is in his secret heart.
The loftiest rewards and opportunities which eternity offers
are not the result of unearned privilege or irresponsible favor-
itism. The highest blessings are only for those people who
have been thoroughly Christlike in their daily living on earth.

In such a tightly-knit group of disciples, word naturally
got around as to what the Sons of Tumult had been asking.
"When the disciples learned of James' and John's request,
they were furious" (Mk.10:41). The record does not state why.
Was it because they had virtuously taken to heart Jesus' recent rebuke about claiming rank, had purged themselves of
selfish ambition, and were now angry because Jesus' cousins

had failed to do likewise? Or were they jealous because the brothers had stolen a march on them and taken unfair advantage of the armistice on power-politics which Jesus had imposed on them? Their subsequent behavior leads one to incline toward the latter explanation.

Whatever the reason, here was a family crisis. So "Jesus summoned them all and said, 'You know that the rulers of the Gentile world govern the common people tyrannically, exercising their power without any judicial restraint. But this is not the way you are to act. Rather, if you want to be important, then minister to human need. If you want to reach the top, you must decide, instead, to serve at the bottom. For the Son of Man's whole purpose in coming is not to be waited on but to serve, giving his life to set men free'" (Mk.10:42-45).

Did this lesson soak into the brothers' minds and hearts? The Gospels do not indicate that it did, but later Scripture and tradition reveal that some time between this event and Pentecost — as with Peter — a divine reversal of motives indeed took place. The quality of their leadership in the infant church proved to be above suspicion. They were honored not for what they were getting out of the Kingdom Crusade but for what they were putting into it. They worked not for self-adulation, but in memory of Jesus and for the glory of God.

The final biblical reference to the Brothers Tumultuous is a happy one. In his round-robin letter to the churches of Galatia, Paul speaks warmly of the two men. He had come to Jerusalem to meet the church leaders and to defend his right to take the Good News to the Gentiles. Of that experience he wrote: "And when they perceived the grace that was given to me, James and Cephas and John, who were reputed to be pillars, gave Barnabas and me the right hand of fellowship" (Gal.2:9 RSV). The Sons of Thunder, who once had sharply forbidden a stranger to act in Jesus' name, now rejoiced in the missionary work of an ex-Pharisee!

IV. What Became of James?

A tradition, which is totally unverified by scriptural sources, strongly ties James to Spain. Under the stimulation of the Holy Spirit at Pentecost the disciple traveled to that country and spent a dozen years or more founding churches and religious communities. Returning to Jerusalem, he became a leader on the home-missionary front, working out of the capital city. Then Scripture again takes up the tale, stating that in the year 37 Herod Agrippa was made king of the Roman territory which included Jerusalem. He curried favor with the religious Establishment by meticulously observing its traditions and customs, and thus more firmly entrenched himself in his position. In 44, in order to further ingratiate himself with the authorities, he launched a brief persecution against the church. Acts declares briefly, "Herod the King laid violent hands upon some who belonged to the church. He killed James the brother of John with the sword; and when he saw that it pleased the Jews, he proceeded to arrest Peter" (Ac.12:1-3 RSV).

Why did Herod Agrippa single out James from among all the disciples for martyrdom? No reason is given. Of course, most of the disciples were scattered widely throughout the Middle East. But it may have been that although the years had tempered James' explosive nature, he still had not forgotten how to thunder, and was thus a natural target. Clement of Alexandria has preserved for us a legend which, though not historically verifiable, might well have been true to the disciple's character. James was arrested, he relates, on the complaint of an enemy. But during the trial, as the accuser watched the saintly demeanor of the disciple, he was moved to accept the new faith. Herod then condemned him to death too. As they were being led to the execution block the new convert knelt before James and asked his forgiveness. James raised him up, said, "Peace be to you," and gave him a forgiving kiss. Then they went forth to martyrdom.

But the legends do not stop here. Even if not probable, they are fascinating, and have been believed by countless thousands of Spaniards, for whom James is the patron saint. For it is written that James' body was returned to Spain and interred in Iria Flavia, appropriately now known as El Padron ("the patron"). The burial-place was lost track of during the Moorish invasion, but was rediscovered by hermits in 813. The body was moved to Santiago de Compostela, "St. James' Field of the Stars." As with Andrew in Scotland, legends tell of James' support in crucial battles to drive the Moors from the country. His final resting-place quickly became the most popular pilgrimage-site for Spaniards in the Middle Ages.

In the early years of America's participation in World War II, death came to a young artilleryman who was a member of a church near one I was serving. After military rites at the grave the minister stepped forward and said quietly to the parents, in my hearing, "I wish with all my heart that your son were still alive. But I am grateful for this — that you have set our community a lofty example of Christlike behavior in facing and accepting this tragedy. And if — God forbid! — any other young man of this city must make the supreme sac- rifice, his family in their bereavement will have the inspiration of your pattern to follow."

James did indeed drink of the cup from which his Master drank. As the first disciple to be martyred, he left an example of courage and faithfulness which may well have heartened his fellow-disciples as they approached and endured their own martyrdoms.

V. What Became of John?

Most of our information about John's later activities comes to us from the Fourth Gospel. Luke tells us that John and Peter were the ones delegated to arrange for the Passover meal (Lk.22:8); but this is the only individual reference in the first three Gospels, whereas John contains six references. Scholars still disagree as to whether the Disciple John wrote the five New Testament books bearing his name, whether they were the work of another person, John the Elder or Presbyter, or whether a series of authors including John contributed to them. The Fourth Gospel, however, when writing about John alone, depicts a gentler side of the bumptious disciple. If John were indeed writing about himself, then we see the more placid inner man; whereas in the three Synoptic Gospels we see the action-prone outer man. Perhaps when the brothers were together they acted as catalysts on one another, causing a tumult which was not present in either when they were apart! Or perhaps by this time John and James had been tempered into mature discipleship under the hammer-blows of the arrest and crucifixion and through the incredulous excitement of the resurrection. For example, we read that at the Last Supper Jesus "was troubled in spirit, and testified, 'Truly, truly I say to you, one of you will betray me.' The disciples looked at one another, uncertain of whom he spoke. One of Jesus' disciples, whom Jesus loved, was lying close to the breast of Jesus; so Simon Peter beckoned to him and said, 'Tell us who it is of whom he speaks.' So lying thus, close to the breast of Jesus, he said to him, 'Lord, who is it?' Jesus answered, 'It is he whom I shall give this morsel, when I have dipped it'" (Jn.13:21-26 RSV). What a different John is portrayed in this vignette from the John who thunderously called for the atomizing of a Samaritan village!

When Jesus was arrested, John's behavior is the best of the disciples'. Having panicked with the rest, he and Peter rallied and followed the detachment of soldiers and their prisoner to the high priest's palace. There John boldly entered the courtyard and shortly thereafter secured entrance for Peter also. But when Peter issued his denials and fled a second time to weep bitterly outside, John alone of them all was left to stand by his Lord (Jn.18:15,16).

His record of faithfulness is enhanced, furthermore, when the four gospels mention no other disciple than himself at the crucifixion. Peter may have watched from a safe distance, but John was right there where his Master could see him. One of the "seven last words of Christ" was spoken directly to him: "Standing by Jesus' cross were his mother, his Aunt Mary who was the wife of Cleopas, and Mary of Magdala. When Jesus saw his mother, and the disciple whom he loved standing beside her, he said, 'Mother, there is your son!' Then he said to the disciple, 'And there is your mother!' From that hour the disciple cared for Mary in his own home" (Jn.19:26,27).

Some years ago in Izmir I was startled to see an official green-and-white traffic sign on the Ephesus road reading "To Mary's House." What greater tribute could Jesus have paid John than to entrust to him the future health and well-being of his mother?

When Mary Magdalene found the tomb empty and reported the mystery to Peter and John, it was not the impetuous Rock who put on an extra burst of speed and came first to the tomb, but the Thunderer! (Jn.20:2-5).

While awaiting Jesus' reappearance in Galilee, the two sets of brothers went back into the fishing business. When Jesus came to them at dawn, Peter swam ashore eagerly to be the first to greet him; but it was the more sensitive John who had first recognized it was Jesus, and had thereby stirred Peter to impulsive action (Jn.21:4-7).

In the Acts John shares with Peter the healing of a cripple, which brings down on them the first taste of persecution.

But with these accounts, historical records end and tradition takes over—writings such as the Acts of John, a wholly fictitious account written by Leucius about 175. More reliable tradition from some of the Church Fathers, however, agrees at a number of points: that John first engaged in missionary activity along the coast of Asia Minor, being based at Ephesus; that during the Emperor Domitian's persecution he was exiled to Patmos, a volcanic island to which minor criminals were sent; that he worked at hard labor for eighteen months; that Domitian's successor permitted him to return and resume his missionary activity; and that a few years later he died in Ephesus of old age. The present Christian community on Patmos, however, insists that John died there; and for proof they show his embalmed body.

Tradition also maintains that he was the only disciple not to die by violence. This is not what his companions would have predicted! The other Thunderer had been beheaded for his zealous leadership, and it was logical to expect John to pay the same price. But history does not always follow a logical course. Tradition further states that as John grew very old, rumors began to arise that his passing would be spectacular. Being an extraordinary man, he would not die in ordinary fashion, but ascend bodily to heaven as his Master had done. Perhaps such rumors had their origin in an incident which closes the Fourth Gospel. Jesus had just told Peter three times, "Feed my sheep." Embarrassed that John had witnessed this interchange, Peter impetuously exclaimed to Jesus, "Yes, Lord, I have your instructions." And jerking a thumb toward John, added, "Now, what about him?"

But Jesus gave him a severe look. "What business is it of yours," he asked, "if I should want him to remain till I come? You are to follow me!" (Jn.21:21,22). The Gospel continues that a rumor then spread widely through the church that John would not die; but hastens to add that it is an inaccurate version of what Jesus had really said.

Yet tradition declares that these rumors persisted and that John was aware of them. So when he felt death approaching, he determined to scotch such rumors for all time. He asked his friends to dig his grave; and when the time came, in the sight of all, he lay down in it, folded his hands and peacefully died. Bryant has described such a placid passing in these familiar lines:

So live, that when thy summons comes to join
The innumerable caravan which moves
To that mysterious realm, where each shall take
His chamber in the silent halls of death,
Thou go not, like the quarry-slave at night,
Scourged to his dungeon; but, sustained and soothed
By an unfaltering trust, approach thy grave
Like one that wraps the drapery of his couch
About him, and lies down to pleasant dreams.

Chapter Five

The Unreported Ones

FULLY half of the disciples have exceedingly thin scriptural dossiers: Philip and Nathanael-Bartholomew, Levi-Matthew and his brother James the Younger, Thaddaeus-Judas and Simon the Zealot. Not being foremost among the Twelve, they were usually eclipsed by the other six. But this does not mean that they were nonentities, nor does it detract from their usefulness to Jesus. Although not often singled out by name, they assumed their share of responsibilties and were represented in all the activities and attitudes which were reviewed in Chapter One. We will consider the first four named above in this chapter, and save Thaddaeus-Judas and Simon the Zealot for Chapter Seven. Perhaps it is fortunate that not all the Twelve were dynamic personalities. Would not Jesus then have had his problems multiplied!

A mother who wanted to enroll her daughter in an Eastern women's college wrote on the admissions application with apprehensive honesty, "Mary Jo is not a leader, but she is a good follower." She need not have worried about being truthful, because the admissions officer replied somewhat as follows: "The admission papers for our incoming class indicate that there are 399 leaders coming to the campus next fall out of 400 openings. We feel that under the circumstances the college is obliged to provide at least one follower. We are happy therefore to accept your daughter's application."

Blessed are those who follow, for without them leaders are useless. And blessed, therefore, are that handful of disciples whose lot it is simply to be undistinguished followers. Apart from improbable legends, we know neither the details of their evangelizing activities, nor the circumstances of their deaths, nor the location of their last resting places. An appropriate epitaph for each, however, is found in the Apocryphal Book of Ecclesiasticus, 44:

> "He was honored in his generation,
>   and was the glory of his times;
> His body is buried in peace,
>   but his name lives forever."

PHILIP

But for the Fourth Gospel we would have no information about this disciple who bears the Greek name meaning "lover of horses." Unfortunately there is another Philip, known as the Evangelist, with whom the disciple is frequently confused. Acts relates that this other Philip was a convert who, along with Stephen and five others, was elected a deacon in the early church. It was he, not Philip the Disciple, who had four marriageable daughters, who evangelized Samaria and baptized the Ethiopian eunuch. This unhappy fact severely limits our knowledge of the fifth person to answer the Master's call. The first three Gospels and the Acts are completely silent about what he thought and said and did; and in John's Gospel there are only four references. These provide the core of our knowledge.

The first episode is as follows: "The next day Jesus decided to go to Galilee. There he found Philip, who was from

Bethsaida, as were Andrew and Peter, and said to him, 'Follow me!'

"At once Philip sought out Nathanael and exclaimed, 'We have found the man about whom Moses wrote in the law, and about whom the prophets spoke! He is Jesus, son of Joseph, from Nazareth.'

"'From Nazareth!' laughed Nathanael. 'Can anything good ever come out of that place?'

"'Come and see!' urged Philip" (Jn.1:43-46).

When one asks, "What is going on here?" several interesting conclusions emerge.

(a) There are two calls to discipleship, both effective. There is Jesus' summons to Philip, and Philip's invitation to his friend on behalf of Jesus. The Fourth Gospel does not record any direct call to Nathanael made by Jesus; perhaps Philip's call proved to be sufficient.

(b) Jesus did not stumble on to Philip by chance and then, being impressed, impulsively add him to the growing band of disciples. Jesus had gone looking for him. This suggests that he had met him earlier, perhaps at one of John the Baptizer's camp meetings. To recruit Philip may have been the major reason for his move just then into Galilee. Although we have no character sketch of Philip, he must have possessed a personal winsomeness and strength which Jesus needed in the men who were to support him. It is unlikely that Jesus would have called into his service anyone whom he felt would be a liability.

(c) Being from Bethsaida, which was primarily a headquarters for commercial fishing, Philip probably fished for a living. This would mean he was acquainted with his competitors, including Peter and Andrew and the two Thunderers, before he was called to be a disciple.

(d) Mark states that when Jesus called these four disciples, they responded by dropping their work at once and following him. The key word is "immediately." Yet when Jesus told

Philip, "Follow me!" Philip must have exclaimed, "Yes, Lord! But first I want to go and find my buddy. I know he will want to join too. It won't take me very long. I'll be right back." And he was.

How different this was from the reaction of the men who were invited to the Great Banquet, the parable which Jesus created on the basis of his own experiences. "A man once invited many guests to a great banquet. As dinner time approached he sent a servant to the guests, saying, 'Everything is ready, so come right away.'

"But with one accord they began offering reasons for not coming. The first one said, 'I have just bought a parcel of land and must go out to examine it. Please excuse me.' Another said, 'I have just acquired five yoke of oxen and am anxious to see how good they are. Please excuse me.' A third said, 'I've just gotten married, and my wife won't let me come'" (Lk.14:16-20).

John Oxenham has captured the message of this parable in these lines:

Lord, I would follow, but —
First, I would see what means that wondrous call
That peals so sweetly through Life's rainbow hall,
That thrills my heart with quivering golden chords,
And fills my soul with joys seraphical.

Lord, I would follow, but —
First, I would leave things straight before I go —
Collect my dues and pay the debts I owe,
Lest when I am gone, and none is here to tend,
Time's ruthless hand my garnering overthrow.

Lord, I would follow, but —
First, I would see the end of this high road
That stretches straight before me, fair and broad;
So clear the way I cannot go astray,
It surely leads me equally to God.

In contrast with the banquet guests, Philip had the kind of excuse which Jesus welcomed — the desire to bring a friend into the Crusade.

(e) Although Philip did not realize it, when he ran to get Nathanael he was not postponing his acceptance of the call, but actually fulfilling it. His action illustrates an individual's instinct to share with others his thoughts and emotions.

Sometimes this appears in undesirable form, as when King Louis XIII of France would drop into a fit of melancholia. He would then throw an arm around a courtier's shoulder, draw him into an alcove and say, "Come, let us be sad together!" Misery loves company. But so also do love and joy and good fortune.

Some years ago a woman in straitened circumstances received a substantial bequest from the estate of a distant aunt. In a tizzy of excitement she lifted the phone, dialed "O" and shrilled, "Operator, get me just anybody!"

For the Christian, this sharing instinct takes the form of commitment to mission, by which the divine purpose is made known to everyone. Philip's search for Nathanael constitutes the earliest home missionary effort recorded in the Gospels, occuring before the Twelve were sent out on their initial field work.

(f) In Jesus, Philip detected more than a random itinerant preacher who needed help in a crusade. He saw him as the latest figure in a significant line of divinely-oriented prophets which began with Moses. Philip did not believe that Jesus just "happened" to appear. Rather, Jesus was the summation of a thousand-year effort on the part of God to make possible the realization of his people's spiritual potential. It was this insight as to the nature of Jesus' ministry which took him hotfooting it to Nathanael; and which commends him warmly to us today.

(g) When Nathanael, gently amused by Philip's en-

thusiasm and his equating of Jesus with the prophets, replied, "Nazareth! When has that village ever produced anything of value?" Philip uttered not one word of argument. So
confident was he of his judgment, and so sure that Nathanael
would find in Jesus the same qualities he had detected, that
he simply grabbed his friend's arm and cried, "Come and
share my experience. Don't look at him through my eyes, but
see him for yourself!"

Is not this the ultimate goal of mission — that no one shall
ever impose on another his concept of Jesus, but rather, that
he shall encourage another to find his own direct, personal
relation with him! Thus Philip might well serve as the Patron
Saint of all missionaries, and all who bear witness to their
fellows of the love of God as made plain in Jesus, in the hope
that they will find it for themselves.

A second biblical episode tells us that "after this Jesus
went to the other side of the Sea of Galilee ... and a multitude
followed him, because they saw the signs which he did on
those who were diseased. Jesus went up into the hills, and
there sat down with his disciples.... Lifting up his eyes, then,
and seeing that a multitude was coming to him, Jesus said to
Philip, 'How are we going to buy bread, so that these people
may eat?' This he said to test him, for he himself knew what
he would do. Philip answered him, 'Two hundred denarii
would not buy enough bread for each of them to get a little'"
(Jn.6:1-3,5-7 RSV). It is difficult to find in this interchange anything
but pessimism. Apparently Philip busied himself thinking
about how much money they did not have while Andrew, as
we have already seen, set the wheels in motion for Christianity's first potluck supper.

Back about 1900 a minister in the Dayton area chanced on
an article about Nostradamus' prophecy that human beings
one day would fly. The author had illustrated his article with
sketches of a flying machine drawn by Leonardo da Vinci. The

minister was incensed at such presumption to attempt what God obviously did not intend man to do. In his eyes this was nothing more than a comtemporary version of Adam's reaching for the forbidden fruit. During the next several years he spent his available time gathering materials under two parallel headings: 1) Why man could not fly, and 2) Why man should not fly. Meanwhile, two Dayton boys went to work on the opposite hypotheses. Today there is an airport at Dayton named for Orville and Wilbur Wright, but there is no church named for the minister. In fact, no one now remembers his name — although "Philip" would not have been inappropriate! For even though Philip is long gone, yet his attitude in that incident — like the smile of the Cheshire Cat — lingers on within the church. How often, as it has been called to meet the unprecedented challenges of our day, has the church elected to follow Philip — when the need has been to follow Andrew!

Was not Jesus really asking his disciple this question: "What are our resources to meet this emergency?" If this were a test, as the Scripture indicates, perhaps Jesus was hoping that Philip would show ability to meet tough situations head-on. If so, Jesus was disappointed, because Philip merely began, like my old Model-T Ford "Jezebel," to vibrate agitatedly in neutral. Screwing up his face in heavy thought, Philip said in effect, "Well, Master, I really didn't know that the situation would ever appear. But now that you ask me, I estimate that it would take fifty dollars to buy enough bread to give everyone one slice — that is, assuming that there are twenty-two slices in each loaf. But where would we ever get that kind of money? O me, O my! And we don't even know where the nearest bakery is. And how would we every transport such a great number of loaves, provided they have that many in stock? I don't see any carts anywhere...."

Just as he was beginning to run down, he was upstaged by

Andrew who came up and said, "Master, there is a lad here...."

While Philip acquitted himself well when first called, in this instance he concentrated so heavily on cataloguing the obstacles — like that Dayton minister — that he had no thought for possible solutions. On the basis of this one incident he might be labeled Philip the Pessimist; but the title is not warranted because there is no other similar incident.

Once, however, he did qualify for the nickname of Philip the Hesitant. "Now among those who had gone up to worship at the festival were certain Greeks. They came to Philip ... and said to him, 'Sir, we want to see Jesus.' So Philip informed Andrew and they went together to tell Jesus" (Jn.12:20-22). We have considered this passage from Andrew's perspective, but now let's ask the recurring question — "What's going on here?" — from Philip's perspective. "Why did Philip not take the foreigners straight to Jesus? Why did he make a detour with them to Andrew first?"

It is possible that the Greeks had approached Philip for the desired introduction because of his Greek name. Did Philip therefore bring them first to Andrew, whose name was also Greek, simply to make the strangers feel more at home? If so, it was a kindly gesture and to his credit.

Or was it merely a neutral gesture, occasioned by Andrew's unexpected appearance just at that moment?

Or did his bringing of Andrew into the situation indicate some insecurity in his makeup?

No one knows for sure, but there is reason to feel that Philip may have had an ulterior motive, the reason for which is easily apparent.

As most Jews of his day, Philip was highly conscious of his status as a member of the Chosen People. He sought, like everyone else, to keep away from the contamination of other peoples and cultures. But these Greeks who had become interested in Jesus were Gentiles, and were rated on the same inferior level as the Samaritans. In Kipling's phrase, they were "lesser breeds without the Law," and might not partake of the joys and responsibilities of God's special promises. What could these strangers from "beyond the pale" want with Jesus? Certainly they could not mean to join the Kingdom Crusade! When Jesus had sent his disciples out on their initial fieldwork, he had warned them explicitly to stay away from Gentiles.

Thus it may have been that Philip was embarrassed by these Greeks who had thrust themselves on him. Certainly he was not delighted with the responsibility of bringing them to his Master. He sought, therefore, to pass the buck to another disciple: "Here, Andrew, you take them to Jesus!" Uncertainty also loves company! But because Andrew apparently felt the same disinclination, they compromised by going together. Each one thus would bear only half of any blame which Jesus or the other disciples might lay on them. If this hypothesis makes sense, it reveals a prudential sort of self-interest rooted in racial prejudice which at times was found in all the disciples, and which has shown up in disciples ever since.

As parochial in outlook as were his compatriots, Philip believed that the Kingdom Crusade was for Jews only. It was natural for him to back away from Gentiles who might show interest, fearing that they might contaminate the purity of the movement. But Philip had overlooked an important lesson from his people's history—namely, that in certain crises they had received important infusions of Gentile blood. One such record is preserved in Matthew's genealogy of Jesus. For amid the listing of all his ancestors there appear the names of four grandmothers who are all Gentiles: Tamar and Rahab the Canaanites, Ruth the Moabite and Bathsheba the Hittite!

Philip did not dream, of course, that the leadership of the Kingdom Crusade would eventually pass into Gentile hands.

He would have been horrified at the thought. But the course of Christian history took that direction, and the Crusade was saved from becoming an ingrowing, strictly Palestinian sect. "God moves in a mysterious way his wonders to perform." Does it not behoove those church people today who anxiously try to keep the fellowship undefiled from any form of expression or leadership unfamiliar to their habits, to be real sure that they are not, instead, irritating the Holy Spirit? For to take the church into protective custody is to strangle it.

John's Gospel provides us with our final biblical episode in which Philip appears.

" 'Do not become fainthearted,' Jesus said. 'Trust in God and have faith in me. My Father's house has many rooms ... and I am going there to prepare a place for you. But even though I am going to make ready for you, I will come again and take you back with me, so that you may be where I am. Already you know where I am going, and how to get there.'

"Thomas exclaimed, 'But Lord, we do not know where you are going, so how can we know the way?'

"Jesus replied, 'I am the Way, the Truth and the Life; no one comes to the Father except through me. If you really knew me you would know my Father also; and from now on you do know him, and have seen him.'

"Philip said, 'Lord, reveal the Father to us. This is all we ask' " (Jn.14:1-8).

Here is that searching, age-old question, "What is God like?" Is he made in our image? How does he behave? What does he expect of us? How can we please him? How may we enlist his aid in time of need? To answer such questions, the world's religions have appeared. So Philip's query was straight to the bull's-eye, expressing the basic hunger of the human soul for firsthand knowledge of the Almighty, and echoing Job's cry, "O that I knew where I might find him!" (Job 23:3). He realized that Jesus' physical life was the servant of his spiritual intentions, which in turn were derived from intimate companionship with God. Philip had seen the fruit of Jesus' strength, but could not find for himself its root. He had not yet become conscious of the indwelling Presence. To him, the Father was still a lovely hued, oblong blur. He sensed that God was not a Cosmic Proposition which could be proved by Euclidean logic, but rather a vital Being who could infuse human personality with love and irradiate individuals with joy. So when Jesus spoke so intimately about his relation to God, all Philip's hunger for similar companionship with the Almighty welled up irrepressibly within him. He burst out, "Show us how to find him. That's all we want."

How fortunate for us that he asked that question! For Jesus replied, "Have I been with you all this time, Philip, without your knowing who I am? How can you say, 'Show us the Father?' when everyone who sees me also sees him?" (Jn.14:8).

Here is a capsule statement of what the Kingdom Crusade sought to reveal about God:

— that when we see Jesus, we also see God;
— that God sent Jesus to reconcile imperfect people to himself;
— that in Jesus we see God's purposes and hopes for his human children revealed in their fullness and glory;
— that as by faith we follow Jesus' example, we walk in the Kingdom's Way, God's Way;
— and that as we are faithful to our Master day-by-day, we shall at last enter into the nearer presense of God, his Father and ours.

On convictions such as these our Christian faith is based. And we are indebted to Philip for the question which has helped to make these convictions clear.

What became of Philip? The Acts and the remainder of the

New Testament are silent. There is nothing but tradition, and some of it — as for example, the "Gospel of Philip," written about 175, is entirely improbable. Eusebius declares that Philip worked to establish churches in Asia Minor and was put to death in Hierapolis. Legendary details as to his final hours are not to be trusted, although his last request is reminiscent of Peter's. He directed that his body not be wrapped in the customary linen, but in papyrus, as he was not worthy to receive the same kind of mortuary preparation which was given his Master.

With the tradition of this final act of humbleness, the doors swing closed on information concerning the fifth disciple.

NATHANAEL BAR-TOLMAI

At Caesarea when Jesus commended Peter for his spiritual perceptivity in proclaiming his Master to be the Christ, the Son of the living God, he used the disciple's full name: "Simon bar-Jona" (Mt.16:17). In Aramaic, "bar" means "son of," a familiar form of identification. Philip would have used it when he said to Nathanael, "The Messiah is Jesus bar-Joseph, from Nazareth."

Now with Nathanael and Bartholomew there is an identification problem which has troubled scholars through the centuries. Four scriptural lists of the disciples include the name of Bartholomew, but John's Gospel never mentions him, naming Nathanael instead, which means "God has given." Most scholars, however, treat the two names as though they belong to but one disciple. Inasmuch as Bartholomew is derived from bar-Tolmai and could have been Nathanael's surname, it is logical to call the sixth disciple Nathanael bar-Tolmai. Yet by whatever name he was known, there is only one scriptural incident in which he is individually identified.

In our survey of Philip we noted that when he was called

he put off following Jesus till he had located Nathanael. He said to him excitedly, "We have found the man about whom Moses wrote in the Law, and about whom the Prophets spoke" (Jn.1:45).

Why should this interest Nathanael bar-Tolmai? There was no particular reason, unless he was a devout believer in the messianic promises and was one who kept himself alert by study and devotions. This means that he could have been almost a ready-made disciple, which Philip sensed.

Nathanael must have tensed with excitement at his friend's words, but then relaxed as Philip continued, "He is Jesus, son of Joseph, from Nazareth."

"The Messiah, from Nazareth!" Nathanael laughed. "Can anything good ever come out of that place?" Some unrecorded folly of its citizens, or their undependable claims to importance, or even some rivalry between Nazareth and Cana, caused Jesus' hometown to be held in amused contempt. It may even have been that Nathanael was quoting a proverb of his day which was similar in meaning to, "Can you get blood out of a turnip?"

But Philip brushed aside this jesting comment as inconsequential and said, "O.K., then, come and see for yourself."

Nathanael's prejudice against Nazarenes must have been superficial because he replied, "Sure, why not? If Philip is wrong," he may have thought, "there's nothing lost. But if he's right...!" He was willing to discard this opinion in favor of a truer one. So the two men hastened back to Jesus who was waiting in the village square, Philip eagerly and Nathanael gently tolerant of his friend's enthusiasm and moderately expectant.

When they approached, Jesus knew that he had seen Philip's friend before. We are not told the circumstances, but apparently Nathanael had been with others under the trees at the edge of the square, and had acquitted himself with credit.

So as he did with Peter, Jesus made an immediate assessment of Nathanael's character. He greeted him by saying, "Here is an Israelite without guile."

Nathanael was startled but also pleased. He asked cautiously, "What makes you so sure?"

Jesus replied, "When you were under that fig tree — remember — before Philip found you, I was watching how you behaved."

The impact of these words on Nathanael, backed as they were by Jesus' vibrant personality, was both immediate and intense. Raised as he had been to say "Thank you" for compliments, he burst out with a more fervent reply than the compliment warranted. In it he compressed his own lightning-like assessment of Jesus, and offered the ultimate affirmation of loyalty and trust: "Why, you're the king of Israel! You're the Son of the living God!" (Jn.1:46-49). He recognized Jesus' messiahship long before Peter did at Caesarea Philippi — and like Peter, all too soon he forgot it again.

The Fourth Gospel records no formal call being extended to this sixth disciple, nor was one apparently needed. What a pity that Nathanael bar-Tolmai did not have the recording services of some young Christian scribe, as Peter had John Mark! Our knowledge of the disciples and the young churches in action around the Mediterranean would have been immeasurably enriched. It is unfortunate, also, that the traditions surrounding him are untrustworthy.

"The Acts of Philip," an unhistorical document, states that bar-Tolmai accompanied Philip to Hierapolis in western Asia Minor. There he survived the persecution which took his associate's life, and escaped to Kurdistan where he founded the Armenian Church. Writing nearly three hundred years after the event, Eusebius declares that bar-Tolmai went to "India" (which could mean any place east of Istanbul), taking with him the Gospel of Matthew, written not in Greek but in

Hebrew. Quite possibly this account is not correct. The apocryphal "Gospel of Bartholomew" is of no help either.

The two divergent legends purporting to recount his death are no more probable. One states that he was martyred in Armenia near the present site of Derbend; whereas the "Apostolic History of Abdias" declares that in "India" priests of the native religion, furious with bar-Tolmai's conversions and miracles, had him beaten and crucified. Such legendary material, though not believed by the modern mind, sought to express lofty praise to this man by showing how he glorified God by being faithful to his Master to the end. And we can add our voices to theirs in appreciation of the quality of Nathanael-Bartholomew's discipleship.

LEVI-MATTHEW

Two other disciples also have been double-named. The First Gospel and Acts call the seventh disciple "Matthew," but Mark and Luke first call him "Levi" and then "Matthew." John's Gospel and the rest of the New Testament do not mention him at all. But there is no doubt that both names refer to the same individual. He and James the Younger had the same father, Alphaeus, about whom nothing is known. The other disciple with duonymic difficulties is Thaddaeus-Judas.

With the calling of Levi-Matthew there was a change in the nature of Jesus' disciples. The first six were fishermen from Bethsaida-Capernaum who were well acquainted with each other. They were a highly homogeneous group. Suddenly without warning Jesus brought in a definitely alien figure. The group was in Capernaum, and we read that "as Jesus passed the customs office he saw Levi, son of Alphaeus, sitting behind the counter.

" 'Follow me!' said Jesus.

"Levi left the booth immediately and became a disciple" (Mk.2:14).

In any century nobody loves an Internal Revenue agent. But in Jesus' day such a man was doubly unpopular because he was in the service of the Roman occupying power. In World War II imagery, Levi was regarded as being a Vidkun Quisling, and was therefore detested by every loyal son of Abraham. By strict Jews he was also regarded as a religious outcast for failure to observe the Law of Moses, and for mingling with other outcasts and foreigners. Thus, it seems curious that Jesus would introduce into his intimate group so controversial a figure. Furthermore, the presence of Levi, in addition to causing bickering among the seven, would certainly raise eyebrows among the "good" people who were watching Jesus' progress with caution. It would also alienate the Establishment which followed with prejudiced eye everything Jesus did. Yet Jesus knew that if his Kingdom Crusade were to reach all classes and kinds of people, such diversity must also be found in the planning and propagating of his movement. It would take more than fishermen to bring in the Kingdom. He called Levi-Matthew, therefore, precisely because of the sort of man he was.

Doubtless Jesus had seen Levi numbers of times, because he often passed the customs tollbooth located on the major road from Damascus, which skirted the Sea of Galilee on its way to the Mediterranean. Levi had purchased from Herod Antipas the right to collect customs fees from every commercial traveler and caravan. He paid a fixed fee for the privilege, collected what he could, and kept the balance. There is no record of any revenue agent operating in the red. This means that he was the wealthiest of all the disciples. But it also means that he had more to give up in joining than did the others. Yet he did not hesitate when Jesus said, "Follow me." He had noticed Jesus before, was aware of his purposes and sympathetic to them. So putting his financial security in peril, he gave the same immediate response which the first six had given—which Jesus somehow had known he would.

John Oxenham concludes the poem earlier quoted with these lines:

> Who answers Christ's insistent call
> Must give himself, his life, his all
> Without one backward look.
> Who sets his hand unto the plow
> And glances back with anxious brow
> His calling hath mistook.
> Christ claims him wholly for his own;
> He must be Christ's, and Christ's alone.

Does not this describe Levi-Matthew? If Jesus' purpose in calling him was to serve notice that the Kingdom was open to persons regardless of class, moral condition or religious status, then Levi gave it full publicity by hosting a banquet for his new Master and associates. The account sounds as though he gave the dinner out-of-doors so that passersby could watch. We read that "shortly thereafter Levi entertained Jesus and his disciples at his home. Other guests included numerous customs agents and similar undesirables who had shown interest in Jesus. Several scribes and Pharisees saw Jesus eating there with the 'dregs' of society, and called out to his followers, 'Why, the very idea! Why does he eat with tax collectors and sinners?'"

The "similar undesirables" were probably not the morally corrupt, but simply the religiously defiled, who made little attempt to observe the 639 Mosaic rules of ceremonial behavior. They were people at odds with the Establishment and therefore, neglected and condemned by it. If they were the dregs of society, they were the religious and political kind, not the socially or ethically degenerate. But even if they had been, would Jesus not have attended just the same? That he was committed to such people is indicated by his reply.

"Overhearing them, Jesus answered, 'Who are the ones

needing a doctor, the healthy or the sick? I am not concerned about good people, but about sinners'" (Mk.2:15-17).

It is important here to notice that Levi gave the feast for the purpose of demonstrating publicly that he was to be identified with the Kingdom Crusade. He was forthrightly standing up to be counted as a disciple, willing to put all his resources at his new Master's disposal. It was his equivalent of receiving baptism, of uniting with a church, or of answering an altar call. It attested to his commitment to the cause, and thereby confirmed Jesus' acumen in calling him to service.

Not every disciple has been gifted with such ability to declare unequivocably his status as a Christian! Nazi Germany produced both cowards and heroes. But people of every age and nation are under the constant pressure of faith to offer crystal-clear evidence of whose they are and whom they obey.

Back in the logging days of northern Wisconsin at the turn of the century the owner of a lumberyard in the southern part of the state was planning to visit one of the rowdiest of the logging camps. Friends tried to dissuade him. "You'd better not go, Clem. Once those lumberjacks find out that you're a deacon in the church and superintendent of the Sunday school, they'll make life tough for you. Preachers who have gone to that camp have been beaten up. So just stay away. It isn't safe."

But Clem replied, "I'll get along all right. It's only for a week."

When he returned a friend stopped him on the street. After looking him over for bumps and bruises, the friend said, "Well, I see that you got back safely. I'm surprised and pleased."

"Oh, I got along fine," Clem said.

"But what did you do come Sunday, when the lumbermen found out that you were a churchman?"

"I just stayed in camp," Clem replied proudly. "They never did find out!"

One can hope that on the following Sunday that man's minister chose to speak about Levi-Matthew who, when he made a commitment, let everyone know in unmistakable fashion, no matter what it might cost him!

In what other ways did Levi-Matthew reveal his total dedication? Alas, trustworthy records are almost non-existent. But there is one tradition of supreme importance because it attaches his name to the First Gospel. Scholars generally agree that Matthew may have collected and transcribed the material in that Gospel which is found there only; and that a later writer took it and the material from the "Q Document"—verses found in both Matthew and Luke—and worked them into the events which Mark by then had chronicled, thus creating Matthew's Gospel in its final form. Christendom thus owes a tremendous debt to this Internal Revenue agent who gave up writing tax reports to Rome in favor of writing a life of Jesus for the whole world.

As with some of the other disciples, the traditions about Matthew's later ministry and death are both contradictory and unbelievable. His area of evangelistic effort was reported positively by different writers as being Judea, Greece, Persia, Turkey, Ethiopia and the area south of the Caspian Sea. One Church Father states that Matthew died of old age, but there are also several mind-boggling legends describing spectacular martrydom. In the light of such diversity and imaginativeness, one is forced to conclude that no one back then really knew anything for sure about Matthew's ministry and death.

He became, as it were, one of those unreported and unheralded heroes, such as the Letter to the Hebrews exalts, "who through faith conquered kingdoms, enforced justice, received promises, stopped the mouths of lions, quenched raging fire, won strength out of weakness" (Heb.11:33,34 RSV). But there is one thing of which we may be sure — that however he may have lived and died, it was in fully committed service to his Master. This is all we really need to know.

JAMES THE YOUNGER

In the Apostolic Church there were three men named James — the Middle English equivalent of the Hebrew "Jacob":

1. James the elder, the third disciple, who was the son of Zebedee, a brother of John and one of the Thunderers; martyred by Herod Agrippa;
2. James the Brother, a later apostle and brother of Jesus, who entered the Kingdom Crusade after the resurrection and became head of the Jerusalem Church; and
3. James the Younger, the ninth disciple, a son of the Mary who was present at the crucifixion, a brother of Levi-Matthew, and of Joses who was a faithful follower of Jesus.

It is this third individual, known also as "the Less" and "the Just" whom we are now considering.

The father of this James was Alphaeus, who is given credit for paternity in various lists of the disciples; but nothing is known about him. Alphaeus' wife and three sons were members of the Kingdom Crusade, but apparently not he. Was he a charter-member of the ancient and worldwide order of men who are content to take their religion secondhand, through their loved ones? What parish caller or pastor has not heard some husband state smoothly, "Oh, I let my wife handle the religion for both of us!" or a father virtuously declares, "I don't need to go myself, but I do see to it that our children are in

church every Sunday. Yes, sir!" Ignoring the fact that neither
his wife nor children can do his religious duties for him, any
more than they can do his eating, sleeping or dying for him,
he sings an inverted version of the old hymn of commitment:

> Take my wife and let her be
> Consecrated, Lord, to Thee;
> Take a dollar now and then,
> But stay away from me. Amen.

Did Alphaeus have this kind of "in-law" relation to the young
church — related to it only by marriage and family? We are not
told.

We know that James' brother Levi-Matthew was a public
servant, a "publican" in Herod Antipas' customs service. What
vocation did James give up? What was his political align-
ment — with Matthew his quisling brother, or with Simon the
Zealot with whom he is grouped? What were the details of his
call? How did he respond? To what country was he assigned
as an evangelist? The answers to all these questions about
James the Younger are lacking.

There is less hard information about this disciple than
about any other. Both Scripture and history are silent. As we
have seen before, tradition is usually so untrustworthy that it
is of little help. According to one legend, he went to Persia to
preach the Gospel and was crucified there. Another relates
that the high priest had him thrown down from the Jerusalem temple into an angry mob which first stoned him and
then beat him to death with clubs. Before his body was
buried it was sawn in two.

How are we to judge between the two legends? One medieval scholar wrote, "In our sober judgment the truth was
never preserved, either as to his manner of ministering or of
his dying." If that is the case, there is no need to choose
between the two legends. But how exciting it would be if

some ancient scroll should come newly to light, an authentic Gospel according to James the Younger! Besides putting scholars into a tizzy, would it not also restore to James much of the stature of which he was deprived through the unexplained silence of the Scriptures?

Chapter Six

Thomas The Libeled

NICKNAMES have been conferred on people in every century. They purport to distill into a word or phrase an epigrammatic appraisal of an individual's character. Whether a nickname is a blessing or a curse depends on how accurate an assessment has been made, and whether it has been prompted by affection or by malice. History is full of nicknames. Consider these variations on "Charles" to be found in France and Spain between the years 689 and 1477:

Throughout the Dark Ages the kings, I'm afraid,
Were nicknamed according to traits they displayed:
There were Charles the Limping and Charles the Fair;
Charles the Bald One without any hair;
Charles the Hammer who drove back the Moor,
Saving all France at the Battle of Tours;
Charles the Crafty and Charles the Mad;
Charles the Simple and Charles the Bad;
Plus two other Charleses: Bold, and Obese —
How glad I'm not "Charles" with nicknames like these!

172

The same practice was observed in England, with such names as Richard the Lion-Hearted, Richard Crookback, and Edward the Confessor who probably did not confess quite everything. The reign of Mary Tudor, daughter of Henry VIII and Catherine of Aragon, produced a nickname which English Protestants will be a long time in forgetting. Because she sought to return her country to the True Faith of Rome by persecution and execution, she was entitled "Bloody Mary." It is inappropriate that even a cocktail should be named after her, because it was not tomato juice that she demanded, but blood.

My favorite nickname, however, is the one bestowed on an early English monarch who was the prototype of unpreparedness. According to the ancient Anglo-Saxon Chronicle, he was not prepared to succeed to the throne; he was not prepared to repel invading Danes; he was not prepared for the treachery of nobles he trusted; and he was not prepared to fight for his throne against Canute the Usurper. Because these failures brought particular misery to England in the Tenth Century, he earned the nickname of "Ethelred the Unready."

But when we come to Thomas the Doubter, it is difficult to believe that he honestly earned this title. Matthew, Mark, Luke and the Acts mention him only when listing the disciples, and John's Gospel contains only three incidents which give insight into Thomas' personality. From these instances one biblical student deduced the following appraisal: "Thomas is represented as a man slow to believe, showing readiness to doubt, seeking the dark side of any question, subject to despondency." If everyone has come to accept this appraisal, then no wonder the disciple is known as "Doubting Thomas." Yet as I examine the same incidents I get quite a different reading of the man.

There was once an ungentlemanly Greek robber giant named Procrustes who had an ingenius way of amusing himself while disposing of his victims. He had two iron beds, one extra long and one extra short. When the victim was too short for the long bed, the robber would stretch him on a rack till he was long enough; and when the victim was too long for the short bed, the robber would saw off his legs. The victim always ended up as a good fit. The "Procrustean bed" has become a much-needed metaphor describing people's efforts to shape truths to their own desires. Indeed biblical passages are sometimes either stretched or edited so as to fit preconceived ideas — in this case, to interpret everything which Thomas said and did in terms of a single lapse from faith.

But because the three instances we have are one hundred percent of what we know about him, he was a doubter in only the opening half of the third incident. This gives him a doubting-record of only 16-2/3 percent, which is better sometimes than ours, and which therefore scarcely makes him eligible for so unfair a nickname! Unfortunately, nicknames are hung on individuals for much less reason than this. But let us review the Gospel record for ourselves.

I. His Courage

In the first incident Thomas showed a greater commitment and courage than did any of the other disciples.

Jesus had been at the Jerusalem temple, teaching in Solomon's Portico. What he had been saying about his Crusade and his relation to God — such as "The Father and I are one" (Jn.10:30) — infuriated the representatives of the Establishment who were listening. At first they heckled him, twice they tried to stone him, and then they attempted to arrest him, but he escaped from Jerusalem and took his disciples northeastward across the Jordan River to a spot where his cousin, John the Baptizer, had first issued his call to repentance. There they would be safe till the furor died away.

John continues: "Now the brother of Mary and Martha of Bethany, whose name was Lazarus, had become deathly ill.

(Mary had been the woman who had poured ointment over the Lord's feet and wiped them with her hair.) The sisters sent a message to Jesus, saying, 'Lord, the man you love is very sick.'

"When Jesus heard the message he said, 'His is not a fatal illness, but one to bring glory to God by revealing the power of his Son.' So even though Jesus loved the two sisters and Lazarus, he stayed right where he was for two more days.

"Then Jesus said to his little band, 'Let us go back to Judea.'"

To the disciples this was the same as putting one's head into a lion's mouth, and they voiced strong objection. "Teacher," they exclaimed, "only a short time ago the people there were trying to stone you. Now you want to go back there again?"

"Jesus replied, 'Our friend Lazarus has fallen asleep, and I am going to wake him up.'

"The disciples said, 'Master, if he has only fallen asleep, then he will wake up by himself.'" There was no need to leave the security of the Transjordanian wilderness.

"Then Jesus told them bluntly, 'Lazarus is dead. I am glad for your sakes that I was not there, so that your faith may be strengthened by what you will see. Let us be on our way'" (Jn.11:1-8,11,12,14,15).

What were the disciples' reactions? Here was a test of their commitment to him. How they responded would reveal what sort of courage they had. He had intimated that their faith would be strengthened if they went. Would this be enough bait to entice them back into the hostile territory so soon after their escape?

The record declares that only one disciple responded, and he was Thomas. While the others shuffled their feet and looked at the ground or the clouds, he acknowledged his readiness to accompany the Master to Bethany: "Thomas, known as 'the Twin,' said to the others, 'All right, let's go, and die along with him!'" (Jn.11:16).

Notice that he spoke not to Jesus but to the disciples. Here was total commitment to his Master, mingled curiously with pessimism. Yet was the pessimism not justified? Was Thomas not putting into blunt words the nagging fear of arrest and execution with which they had so recently been threatened? "Come on, you scaredy-cats!" he said in effect. "Let's stand by him. Sure, we may be putting our necks in a noose. But the Master has work to do in Bethany." His was a dedicated spirit in spite of danger.

In 1882 when authorities in the Black Hills decided to apprehend the Axelbee gang of outlaws, Cap and Fred Willard, lawmen from Deadwood, and Jack O'Hara, the Sheriff of Spearfish County, rode northwest to Stoneville in Montana Territory. They were aware that they would be outnumbered two to one, so each sought to give the other a sense of being supported. When the battle was over, Sheriff O'Hara lay on the ground mortally wounded. As the Willard brothers knelt beside him, he gasped, "I came to stand beside you, Cap, and I stayed as long as I could."

Was it not in something of this spirit that Thomas both challenged and shamed the other disciples into standing by their Lord? Here was no "readiness to doubt," no indication that he was "subject to despondency." Quite the contrary! The anonymous student who suggested that it does was trespassing perilously near the precipitous escarpment of verbal inexactitude!

So it was that the disciples returned with Jesus to his ministry, eleven of them reluctantly. From time to time they may have looked uneasily back over their shoulders, half-expecting to find the high priest's minions in hot pursuit. But as a reward for their continuing faithfulness — for which at this juncture Thomas was responsible — they not only saw Lazarus restored to life but they were also privileged to hear some of the most treasured words which Jesus ever uttered: "I am the resurrection and the life. Anyone who dies believing in me shall live again; and anyone who lives out his faith in me shall never die" (Jn.11:25,26).

Significantly, the incident concludes with the Establishment discussing what should be done about Jesus. After listening impatiently to the tentative suggestions of various council members, that year's high priest, Caiaphas, exclaimed, "'You are speaking stupidly, not realizing what is at stake. Otherwise you would see that it is to our advantage to have but one man bear the whole burden of Rome's punishment, rather than to have the entire nation destroyed.' So from that day forward they considered means of having him killed" (Jn.11:49,50,53).

Was not Thomas being more realistic than pessimistic, then, when he exclaimed to the unwilling eleven, "Let's go with him, even if it be to death!"

II. His Commitment

In the second incident Thomas' deep commitment produced one of his Master's most memorable teachings.

Jesus had warned the disciples that one of them would soon betray him, and then said, "I give you a new commandment—love one another. Just as I have loved you, so you are to love one another. If you can do this, everyone will recognize that you are indeed my disciple" (Jn.13:34,35). He followed this with a forecast of Peter's denials, but added, "Do not become faint-hearted. Trust in God and have faith in me. My Father's house has many rooms—would I be saying this if it were not so?—and I am going there to prepare a place for you. But even though I am going to make ready for you, I will come again and take you back with me, so that you will be where I am. Already you know where I am going, and how to get there."

"Thomas exclaimed, 'But Lord, we do not know where

you are going, so how can we know the way?'" (Jn.14:1-5).

Was Thomas just being stupid, or was he merely confused? Was his reply blackly pessimistic, as some critics have suggested, implying that hope for the future was futile? I do not detect such overtones. Rather, Thomas seems to be honestly perplexed. Reading back through earlier verses, one sees that Jesus had said several seemingly contradictory things. He had said, "Where I am going you are not able to come" (Jn.13:53). Peter asked for clarification, "Lord, where are you going?" and was told, "You cannot follow me to where I am going; but you will follow later on!" (Jn.13:56). The question was not answered and nobody was any the wiser. So when Jesus continued, "Already you know where I am going, and how to get there" (Jn.14:4), the disciples must have looked at one another quite confusedly.

The Gospels speak of occasions when the disciples did not understand what Jesus was saying, but acted as though they did because they were afraid to admit being obtuse. Here was another instance in the making, till Thomas decided he would act that way no longer. Committed fully to the Kingdom Crusade as he was, he was upset because he must have missed some truth vital to his future. His life with Jesus was bound up in this teaching, whatever it was. There is a hymn in which a line is frequently repeated, "Sometime, sometime we'll understand." Thomas would have had no use for it. He wanted to know fully, right now!

His attitude was in sharp contrast to that of the Primitive Baptist preachers at the turn of the century. Totally illiterate and untrained, they prided themselves on how unenlightened they were, for then whatever they said or did would be at God's orders, and give him greater glory. Bob Childress, himself a Blue Ridge mountain pastor, told of hearing one such preacher bellow, "Praise be to God that I am ignorant. I would only praise him more if I were ignoranter!" But this is preposterous poppycock. What an excuse for laziness! In his Beecher Lectures on Preaching Charles Sylvester Horne stated, "Let me lay it down that there is nothing in Holy Writ to warrant the assumption that a man is likely to be more spiritual if he is an ignoramus; or that prophetic power in the pulpit especially attaches to the preacher whose heart is full and whose head is empty."

A southern sharecropper stopped hoeing one morning and thought, "The sun is so hot, the weeds are so tough and my back is so sore — that I feel a call to the ministry!" And yet, by contrast, Jesus demanded of his followers the maximum use of their brains: "Love God with all your heart, with all your soul, with all your mind and with all your strength" (Mk.12:30). Dr. Horne later added, "The church of today needs to ponder deeply on this fact, that it was the man of most massive intellect and most varied scholarship who was the first Christian evangelist." It is no wonder then that for scores of years most of the major denominations have insisted that ordained ministers be graduates of accredited four-year colleges and three-year seminaries. Harvard College was founded to ensure the continuation of an intelligent and scholarly ministry for New England. Graven on the Johnston Gate is this inscription:

> After God had carried us safe to New England, and we had builded our houses, provided necessaries for our livelihood, reared convenient places for God's worship and settled the civil government, one of the next things we longed for and looked after was to advance learning and perpetuate it to posterity, dreading to leave an illiterate ministry to the churches when our present ministers shall lie in dust.

An ignorant leadership is an affront to both God and man. Apparently Thomas held the same idea.

Thus one may be sure that when Thomas asked to be enlightened, Jesus nodded approval while making a simple yet comprehensive reply. "I am the Way, the Truth and the Life. No one comes to the Father except through me" (Jn.14:6). In effect, Jesus was saying to them, "I will soon be with my Father. The road to his house of many rooms is the one I am now walking. If you want to reach those rooms, you must follow in my footsteps. Your loyalty to me will set your feet on the right path. Therefore, I am the Way." Having lived life to the full, Jesus was well aware of its excitement and its routine, its joys and its sorrows, its brutality and its glory. Because he knew it so thoroughly, he was competent to guide others safely through it into his Father's nearer presence.

"Your acceptance of my teachings," he continued in effect, "gives you the will to keep traveling in that Way. Therefore I am the Truth." Because Jesus' precepts are as integral a part of the cosmos as mountains and molehills, we can practice those teachings in the confident assurance of God's support. "The stars in their courses fight against Sisera."

"The eternal life which I am to receive will be yours also," he concluded, "when you are faithful to me. Therefore I am the Life." The incentive for prizing immortality and the dynamic for achieving it are in Jesus, ready to be appropriated by those who continue to follow him.

What reassurance these words have brought to stumbling disciples everywhere! For example, in the year 155 persecution broke out in Smyrna (now Izmir, Turkey), and a number of Christians were put into the arena to fight wild beasts. Eventually the crowd demanded that the bishop, whose name was Polycarp, be brought to the stadium. The arresting officer, who respected the old man, said to him coaxingly, "What's the harm in offering a pinch of incense and saying 'Lord Caesar'?" But Polycarp shook his head. As they entered the stadium a great roar went up from the waiting crowd, but above it all the bishop heard a voice from heaven, saying, "Be strong, Polycarp, and play the man!" He was led to the box of the proconsul who, out of respect for his age, said, "Swear by the genius of Caesar; curse the Christ and I will let you go."

Polycarp replied, "Eighty-six years I have served him, and he has done me no wrong. How then can I blaspheme my king who has saved me?"

The crowd then cried out, "Polycarp to the lions!" but the Proconsul ordered that he be burned at the stake. As the wood piled high about him he prayed, "I give thee thanks that thou hast counted me worthy of this day and this hour, that I should have a part in the number of thy martyrs in the cup of thy Christ, to the resurrection of eternal life." And he played the man to the end.

It is good therefore for us to remember but that for Thomas' hunger to know fully about the Good News, these words about "the Way, the Truth and the Life" might never have been spoken. And how much the poorer we then would be!

III. The Doubting Incident

In the final instance, Thomas moved from normal doubt to complete faith. In this he was no different from any other disciple.

We have already seen that in instance after instance all the disciples first met the claims and evidences of Jesus' resurrection with incredulity and unbelief. Luke, for example, relates that while they were still discussing the unbelievable report of the two men from Emmaus, "Jesus himself appeared among them. Supposing that he was a ghost, they pulled back from him in fright. But he said, 'Why are you so upset and confused? You can see from my hands and feet that it is really I. Touch me and see, for ghosts do not have the flesh and bones that I do.' And because joy and wonder still fought with unbelief within them, he spoke again, 'Do you have anything to eat?'

"They gave him a piece of broiled fish; and while they watched he ate it" (Lk.24:36-43).

Here was a four-fold pattern: the disciples were incredulous; they were told to look at the nail marks on his hands and feet; they were invited to touch him to prove that he was real; finally they were convinced. But how were they any more "doubting" than Thomas, who got his nickname from following almost the identical pattern of incredulity, examination and belief? John's account might even be a variant version of Luke's, with Thomas, not the Eleven, in the leading role. For consider how John writes that Mary had brought word of the empty tomb, and then continues:

"On the evening of that day, the first day of the week, the doors being shut where the disciples were for fear of the Jews, Jesus came and stood among them and said to them, 'Peace be with you.' When he had said this, he showed them his hands and his side. Then the disciples were glad when they saw the Lord. Jesus said to them again, 'Peace be with you. As the Father has sent me, even so I send you.' And when he had said this, he breathed on them and said to them, 'Receive the Holy Spirit. If you forgive the sins of any, they are forgiven; if you retain the sins of any, they are retained.'

"Now Thomas, called the Twin, one of the Twelve, was not with them when Jesus came. So the other disciples told him, 'We have seen the Lord!' But he said to them, 'Unless I see in his hands the print of the nails, and place my finger in the mark of the nails, and place my hand in his side, I will not believe'" (Jn.20:19-25 RSV).

The account continues, "Eight days later his disciples were again in the house, and Thomas was with them. The doors were shut, but Jesus came and stood among them and said, 'Peace be with you.' Then he said to Thomas, 'Put your finger here, and see my hands; and put out your hand, and place it in my side; do not be faithless, but believing.'

"Thomas answered him, 'My Lord and my God!'" (Jn.20:26-28 RSV).

In Tennyson's "Idylls of the King," Sir Gareth describes an ecstatic experience in which he exclaims, "I leapt from Satan's foot to Peter's knee!" The change within Thomas was that radical, just as with the ten disciples in Luke's account. They were one together both in their doubting and in their believing. Thus if there is any doubt that Thomas was more doubting than the rest, let us give him the benefit of the doubt!

IV. The Value of Honest Doubt

It is not wise to be hasty in condemning honest doubt anyway. Jesus did not rebuke Thomas for rejecting for a time an illogical belief in his Master's resurrection. Honest doubt is far more healthy both to body and soul than pious gullibility. More damage is wrought through religious credulousness than by genuine questioning. What a pity that Christianity must continually be defending her virtue against some of her followers! Yet this is necessary because so much of the stupidity which is offered today under the guise of faith is being snapped up by the gullible. Honest doubt is the most effective instrument with which to meet this challenge and keep the faith pure and undefiled. Indeed, is it not one of the mainsprings of authentic progress in every area of life? Take religion as an example. Through the centuries the Faith has been plagued by heretical and almost blasphemous notions about the will of God. These have been overcome only by the honest doubts of believers.

An appeal to God's will has been used to excuse human wickedness. The book, *The Man Who Moved a Mountain* describes a funeral sermon given by a Primitive Baptist preacher

at the grave of a young drunk who had tried to kill his stepmother and had shot himself instead:

> "Little Georgie-a, is a-walkin' the streets of glory-a.
> He done exactly what the Lord wanted him to do-a.
> When the Lord pulled the foundations of the world-a,
> He planned for little Georgie to be born-a,
> And to get drunk-a, and to try to shoot his stepmother-a,
> And to have the pistol go off and shoot himself-a.
> And he fulfilled God's purpose-a,
> And he's gone the way that God wanted him to go-a."

This, of course, is pagan fatalism in the name of religion. And
when people began to entertain honest doubts about this
belief and turned to the Scriptures for verification, they rediscovered God as revealed by Jesus, and purged the faith of a
gross error.

God's will has also been blamed for human illness. When I
was young, the number one and two killers of children were
diphtheria and smallpox. Graveyards around the world are
full of small tombstones with sad lines such as these:

> "Here lies
> Little Kent;
> God called,
> And he went."

Yet doctors and scientists had honest doubts about God be-
having so callously. They began to say, and finally to shout,
"Diphtheria and smallpox, polio and meningitis do not afflict
humankind by the will of God. Rather, they come in defiance
of that will. We are going to see that these scourges are wiped
out so that God's will may be fulfilled for his children without
interference!" Today therefore when a case of diphtheria is
found anywhere in the United States, the Public Health Service counts it a disgrace. Our country has finally been able to

cancel its requirement that citizens returning from abroad must show proof of a valid smallpox vaccination. In all countries this former despoiler of the will of God has been conquered, thanks to honest doubt.

The death penalty for sin has similarly been attributed to God's will. In my hearing a minister once read aloud to a group of young people the story of Achan who, instead of turning over to Joshua all the loot he had obtained from the conquest of Ai, as the Lord had commanded, had hidden some silver, gold and a cloak in his tent. The account concludes with the execution not only of Achan but also his family and livestock. "All Israel stoned him with stones; they burned them with fire, and stoned them with stones.... And the Lord turned from his burning anger" (Josh.7:25,26 RSV). After closing the Bible the minister slowly shook his head. "It seems hard to believe that God would command that the whole family be put to death, just because of the father's greed."

But his wife snorted and said crisply, "Of course it was God's will. He had to make an example of Achan's family that would be so severe that it would make everyone else obedient."

But there are many believers who have had honest doubts that God would enforce his will by such monstrous methods. Indeed, is not God himself the source of these doubts, if for no other reason than to clear his name of infamy!

If, therefore, one still insists on labeling Thomas the "Doubter," let him credit Thomas with the kind of honest doubting which keeps the truth undefiled!

From this point on we must depend on non-biblical tradition for information about Thomas. There are two variant versions. Eusebius' *Church History*, dating from about the year 350, declares that Parthia—the greatly enlarged Persian Empire—was assigned to Thomas for evangelizing. Later sources declare that he was martyred in Edessa, Syria, and that a great church was built there in his memory.

The other version, drawn from the historically unreliable "Acts" and "Gospel" of Thomas and other late sources, states that Thomas took the Good News to a whole string of peoples from Mesopotamia eastward and died in Calamina, India. At one time Parthia extended from the Tigris to the Indus rivers so that he might have worked in part of today's India while being in the Parthia of his day. The Mar Thoma Church, an ancient and highly-respected body of Christians centered in Malabar and Kerala claims that Thomas was its founder. Because of Hindu jealousy over his success in winning converts, he was speared to death on a high hill near Madras, now known as Mount Thomas. According to the Scottish scholar, William Barclay, the Portuguese explorer Vasco da Gama discovered numerous Christian relics at the site, including an ancient chapel beneath which were bones of such brilliant whiteness that da Gama piously concluded that they must be Thomas's. The Portuguese built a shrine to mark the place. Thus Thomas has two final resting-places, and his special day in the calendar of saints is December twenty-first.

John's third account, which we have reviewed, depicting both Thomas's skepticism and his belief, closes with unforgettable words of commendation from his Master. Thomas uttered his acceptance of the Risen Christ with his reverent words, "My Lord and my God!" Jesus replied, "Have you believed because you have seen me? Blessed are those who have not seen and yet believe." (Jn.20:29 RSV). With these words he blesses us today who have as great a temptation to be "Doubting Thomases" as that disciple. And as a distant echo of confirmation come the words of Peter's First Letter: "Though you do not now see Jesus, you believe in him and rejoice with unutterable and exalted joy. As the outcome of your faith you obtain the salvation of your souls" (1 Pe.1:8,9 RSV).

Having lived with Jesus but never having believed in his resurrection till conviction was forced on him, Thomas was able to find a rich fulfilment of his life in spreading the Good News. In like manner, when an individual today who has never seen Jesus learns to exclaim with Thomas, "My Lord and my God!" he will be empowered to become his Master's servant in the service of men.

Chapter Seven

The Overzealous Three

THE other double-named disciple is Thaddeus-Judas. In Matthew's and Mark's list of disciples he appears in tenth position (and in Matthew he is also called Lebbaeus), but in Luke-Acts and the Fourth Gospel he is called Judas, son of James. A few scholars hold that Thaddeus and Judus were two separate people, but because most scholars can find no good reason against it and because so little information about either man is available, they follow the simplest route of calling this tenth disciple by both names.

In the entire New Testament the spotlight falls just once on this man, the "good" Judas. During the Last Supper Jesus promised that the disciples would receive the comfort and inspiration of the Holy Spirit, and added, "'I will not utterly desert you, for I will return to you. Shortly the world will see me no more, but you will see me. Because I live, you will live also. Then you will know that I am one with my Father and that you are one with me and I am one with you. He who knows my commandments and obeys them is the one who truly loves me; and he who thus loves me will be loved by my Father. I, too, will love him and make myself known to him.'

"Judas (not Iscariot) asked him, 'Lord, what is the reason for your making yourself known to us but not to the world?'" (Jn.14:18-22).

This was a pertinent question. Jesus had been talking about his future return in glory, and had said that he would be recognized and accepted only by those who love him. So Thaddeus-Judas asked, "Why don't you make yourself known to everybody spectacularly, instead of just quietly to us? We know you already, and the world doesn't. Isn't that the whole idea of the Kingdom Crusade? Don't you want to see the earth filled with the glory of God? You have the powers of the Almighty behind you; why don't you use them?"

Because Thaddeus-Judas has also been called a Zealot, it may be assumed that he and Simon the Zealot saw eye-to-eye about the future. It was strikingly different from the future Jesus contemplated. The two were committed to a strongly nationalistic vision wherein the Jews regained their independence through a crushing defeat of the Roman legions, thus permitting the blessings of God to descend again freely upon his people. Apparently Thaddeus-Judas had expected Jesus to take the leading role in this denouement, and must have been shocked when Jesus would make himself known only to a relatively small handful of people—those who loved him.

The challenge to fill Thaddeus-Judas' expectations of a violent military-political coup as the proper way to conduct his ministry was no new idea to Jesus. Luke relates that "full of the Holy Spirit Jesus left the Jordan and was sent by the Spirit into the wilderness for forty days, where he was tempted by the devil."

The devil's opening temptation was this: "Concentrate on caring for people's physical needs. Feed them, heal them, clothe them, amuse them, and you'll have them in your pocket. They will give you everything you want." The second temptation was: "Trade spiritual authority for political power.

The masses cheer a popular dictator and blindly obey his will. They'll do anything you ask!" The third temptation was: "Concentrate on the spectacular! Constantly wow people. Keep them breathless with anticipation as to what amazing thing you will do next. Then you've got them!" Then the temptation narrative ends, "Having by then run out of temptations, the devil went away, resolving to return at a more opportune time" (Lk.4:1-13).

One such time was the occasion when Thaddeus-Judas put the second temptation before him again. But Jesus patiently replied, "The man who loves me will follow my teachings. My Father will love him, and we will come to him and dwell in his heart. But the man who does not love me will ignore my teachings — which are not mine, after all, but which belong to the Father who sent me" (Jn.14:23,24). He was saying in effect, "Look, Thaddeus, it is not God's Will that I become the kind of Messiah you want. My kingdom cannot be proclaimed spectacularly from the temple-top, with everyone shouting for joy and destroying his enemies. Not at all! Mine is a Kingdom of love which spreads by the contagious contact of one heart with another. My Kingdom is extended not by unholy insurrection, but by holy affection. It can reach worldwide proportions this way, just as you want. Remember the Parable of the Mustard Seed! My way is the only way the Kingdom can spread. It is up to you, therefore, Thaddeus, and every one of my followers, to live in that Kingdom of love here and now, so that as you continue my ministry the contagion of love becomes an epidemic. Then, and not till then, will your dreams of a world at peace come true!"

> "For not with swords loud clashing,
>   Nor roll of stirring drums;
> With deeds of love and mercy
>   The heavenly kingdom comes."

How well did Thaddeus-Judas learn this lesson? We do

not know. One tradition declares that after Pentecost he went to Edessa with the Good News. There King Abgar believed that he was the emissary which Jesus earlier had promised to send. Abgar was healed of his leprosy, and he with his whole court were baptized into the faith.

Another tradition declares that he went to Armenia, and eventually to Kurdistan where he was killed with arrows.

More than this we do not know, except this—that he shares with Bartholomew today the love and affection of Armenian Christians.

SIMON THE ZEALOT

While perhaps six of the disciples were fishermen and one a customs collector and therefore all seven conservatives, at least three are thought to be of radical stripe: the three considered in this chapter. A Zealot was more than just a person of unrestrained commitment who showed an un-common amount of zeal for whatever movement claimed his loyalty. This broad meaning is found in the Psalmist's cry, "Zeal for your house has eaten me up!"—which verse kept young Theodore Roosevelt home from church once because he was afraid of being eaten by the "zeal!" When relating this in later years he observed drily that the church was now safe for small children because much of the "zeal" was gone!

If mere enthusiasm were the mark of a Zealot, we could understand why Jesus wanted three of them among his dis-ciples. They would serve as sparkplugs to fire his whole group and get them on the road, "hitting on all twelve!"

But instead the Zealots were members of a fiery "Go home, Romans!" revolutionary party first organized by Judas of Gamala to oppose the census of A.D. 6. The first census had been at the time of Jesus' birth, when Quirinius was governor of Syria from 6 to 4 B.C. Because it had been carried out by Jewish authorities according to tribes and clans, it elevated nobody's blood-pressure.

But then King Herod died and his kingdom was brought directly under Roman rule with Quirinius as ruler. When he ordered a second census, this time to be taken by Roman authorities to update their tax records, riots broke out. It was not only because of resentment against "taxation without representation," but also because the Jews believed that only their own leaders, under God's authority, had the right to levy taxes. Resenting keenly the loss of their last vestige of independence, they regarded the census as Quirinius's effort to discover how many "slaves" Rome had available in the new province.

Then it was that Judas of Gamala organized his guerrilla party of fiercely nationalistic insurrectionists, known as the *Zelotes*. For several months he conducted a reign of terror, killing both Romans and any Jews suspected of having fraternized with the enemy. It was analogous to the Mau-Mau uprising in East Africa. Finally Judas was captured and executed, and the movement went underground, smoldering along through the years like a burning lignite mine and drawing into membership the hotheads, the social misfits, the religious outcasts and the outright brigands, all of whom needed some machinery into which to feed their heads of super-charged steam. Barabbas was probably a Zealot. The tragedy of the movement is that the violence it employed as a means to free the country ultimately destroyed the nation in the year 70. Jesus knew that violence is its own worst enemy, and would never have become a Zealot. But he had high hopes that three members of that group would make good disciples, and he batted .666.

Simon found himself at home therefore with both the "good" Judas and the "bad" Judas; but one wonders what kept him from slipping the assassin's knife into Matthew-Levi who in his eyes was a dirty traitor! And how did he get along with the fisherfolk who very likely paid little attention to the political news? Although we are never told how these war hawks got along in the circle of doves, at times each of the disciples must have felt that he was enduring strange bed-fellows.

What did Simon the Zealot have to say about it himself? Well, the fact is that not one particle of information as to his sayings and doings is recorded in Scripture! This peculiar silence which comes close to engulfing at least half of the disciples smothered this man completely.

The only answer that might possibly explain such silence appears to be this: that although the righteousness of the Zealots' cause was acknowledged by many Jews, few joined the party because of its terrorist activities. Many regarded the objective as good, but the means of achieving it bad. Furthermore, those who were influential in the religious and political Establishments were actually opposed to the Zealots because the party continually endangered the status quo which those authorities strove to maintain in order to pre-serve their few remaining powers and privileges.

Little wonder, then, that the young church, as it de-veloped its own life under the Roman umbrella independent from synagogues and temple, did not wish to upset any applecarts, particularly Roman ones. Persecution hung too close to its head as it was, without the Romans learning that on Jesus' staff had been three of the dangerous *Zelotes*. If this were in fact the case — which we do not know — might not the leaders of the church have tried to soft-pedal any insurrec-tionist influence in their midst, concealing with blackout cur-tains the fact that a quarter of their Founder's original disci-ples were revolutionaries?

What may have been Jesus' motive in calling Simon to follow him? It does not make sense if Jesus wanted a homo-genized group of quiet-mannered disciples. But if he wanted a cross-section of the poor, the outcast, the dispossessed as disciples, who treasured the Kingdom and were willing to work faithfully for it, then did he not need the enthusiasm and zeal of a Simon who believed passionately in the coming of a Messiah? Could he not also use a man who had defied Rome in order to restore independence to his nation — not an independence which the Zealots would exploit for themselves, but which would make possible the restoration of God's rule through divine laws? For Jesus was trying to restore that divine rule, not through Moses' outdated Law but through a New Covenant as promised by Jeremiah: "I will put my law within them, and I will write it upon their hearts; and I will be their God, and they shall be my people. And no longer shall each man teach his neighbor and teach his brother, saying, 'Know the Lord,' for they shall all know me, from the least of them to the greatest" (Jer.31:33,34 RSV). But, unfortunately, to such questions as these the Scriptures give no answers.

The silence about Simon is broken only by the inclusion of his name in all five lists. We know, therefore, that he stuck with the group after the crucifixion and the dashing of his hopes that Jesus would be a militant Messiah. He must have learned through the ressurrection that the power of God's love was greater than a human enemy's violence, and come to accept that truth for himself. Otherwise, would he have stayed with the disciples, preaching that truth and eventually dying for it?

Legend supports this possiblity, for it links Simon and Thaddeus-Judas in a mission to Persia. Other traditions also make him quite a globetrotter, serving in Egypt, Africa, Armenia, Jerusalem and even England! He and Thaddeus were about to be killed in a temple filled with jeering enemies when an angel gave them the choice of escaping by collapsing the temple with great loss of life, à la Samson the Playboy — or of suffering their imminent fate. Both men refused so great a price for their lives and so were martyred. What a change had occurred in this disciple who earlier might have murdered his own parents without compunction, but who now rejected violence against those about to kill him! Simon the Zealot had come a long way in understanding and pleasing his Master!

JUDAS THE TRAGIC

The twelfth disciple was Judas, the son of Simon of Kerioth. Although his name means "worthy to be praised," he has a firm hold on last place in the scriptural lists. Kerioth was a border town in the northeast corner of Judea, and it is likely that Judas was the only southerner among the disciples. He may have become known as the "Man from Kerioth" (Iscariot) to distinguish him from Thaddeus-Judas.

A. His Characterization

Everyone hates a traitor, so the memory of Judas has received especial opprobrium through the centuries. The "Arabic Gospel of the Infancy" even states that the evil in him was present in his youth, but this record is not to be trusted. For multitudes of people he represents the epitome of wickedness. Yet the scriptural record affords at least two surprises.

Originally he must have been a promising candidate for discipleship, or Jesus would never have called him into service. Not only was his messianic enthusiasm contagious, but so also his entire personality.

He must also have possessed "an honest face," appearing as a man above suspicion whom everyone trusted. The demonic potential was so deeply submerged beneath his angelic potential that the other disciples never dreamed that he would eventually betray the Kingdom Crusade. He shared their daily life in ordinary fashion, giving no warning either in attitude or behavior of any crucial defect of character. That he was regarded as a man of honor is evident for two reasons.

First, his fellow-disciples made him their treasurer. He handled the common purse into which went all contributions, and from which all expenses were paid. He held the equivalent of the office of steward.

Second, as his decision to betray Jesus matured, only Jesus came to realize it. And when even he gave general warnings, none of the disciples suspected Judas.

Judas was also identified with the Zealot movement. This meant that he was a fanatic regarding Israel's political future. He had entered the Kingdom Crusade on the assumption that Jesus was his kind of Messiah, one who would eventually lead a miliary campaign to drive the Romans into the sea and make possible the political revolution which would toss out the Jews who had collaborated with Rome, creating a fresh new state. Being fanatical on this point as he was, Judas could have been secretly "unhinged" in other areas. Jesus may have felt that in adding Judas to his group he was taking a calculated risk, hoping that the man's energy and devotion would counterbalance his emotional instability. He may also have hoped that Judas' vociferous enthusiasm would stimulate the hopes and visions of the others. Yet Jesus was no innocent dreamer, for the Fourth Gospel indicates that if one of the disciples were to give way under pressure, Jesus knew who it would be (Jn.6:64).

That Judas was not pressure-resistant is indicated by the fact that he backslid from his two favorable character-traits. The attractive candidate for discipleship, the popular young enthusiast for the Kingdom Crusade gradually changed into a morose, secretive individual capable of theft and betrayal. He came into the movement with a high promise, openhearted and zealous; he left it disappointed and disillusioned, a tragically altered man.

And he similarly backslid from the integrity which had

once been obvious and became an embezzler. Undoubtedly the son of a poor peasant — for it was the down-trodden and the dispossessed who had nothing to lose and everything to gain who became Zealots — Judas had known few opportunities to handle money and enjoy the excitement of feeling drachmas between his fingers. That this experience of being group treasurer provided first a temptation and then an irresistible opportunity is indicated in John's Gospel.

While Martha was serving supper to Jesus and the disciples in Bethany, "Mary took a pound of costly ointment of pure nard and anointed the feet of Jesus and wiped his feet with her hair; and the house was filled with the fragrance of the ointment. But Judas Iscariot, one of the disciples (he who was to betray him), said, 'Why was this ointment not sold for three hundred denarii and given to the poor?' This he said, not that he cared for the poor, but because he was a thief, and as he had the money box he used to take what was put into it" (Jn.12:3-6).

It was Judas' tragedy, then, that over a period of months he reversed Sir Gareth's experience, and fell from Peter's knee to Satan's foot! For the day came when he went to the authorities and promised to take them to the place where Jesus could be arrested while alone, with no crowds to interfere. This constituted the betrayal.

We learn that Judas took the fateful steps directly after Jesus had rebuked him for criticising Mary's "waste" of the ointment. This apparently was the last straw. "Then one of the disciples, who was called Judas Iscariot, went to the chief priests and said, 'What will you give me if I deliver him to you?' And they paid him thirty pieces of silver. And from that moment he sought an opportunity to betray him" (Jn.26:14-16 RSV).

There are two other biblical references to this amount of money, which was about twenty dollars: (1) "If an ox gores a

slave, male or female, the owner shall give to his master thirty
shekels of silver, and the ox shall be stoned" (Ex.21:32 RSV); (2) It
is also the wages of the Worthless Shepherd (Zech.11:12).

B. Possible Reasons for the Betrayal

Why did Judas commit this act of betrayal? There are at
least five answers to the question, of varying acceptability.

The first states that the entire blame rests not on Judas
but on Jesus. For he, so the argument runs, had foreknowledge that his death was inevitable and required. It was necessary, therefore, for Jesus to include in his party one who
would betray him to the executioner. This explanation, reminiscent of bad medieval theology, cannot be supported by
Scripture.

A second answer also frees Judas from culpability, but
substitutes God for Jesus as the cause. God foreordained his
Son's death as a penalty for the world's sin and as a means of
grace; and Judas was an innocent tool of the divine will. One
competent scholar's reaction to this explanation is the one
word, "Blasphemy!"

A third answer makes the blame rest on Judas, but only
lightly. He is given expiatory credits for having had the best of
intentions; he "meant well." His purpose in betraying Jesus
was not to send him to his death — God forbid! — but to force
his master to use his superhuman powers to save himself. In
so doing, Jesus would stop being an ineffectual Suffering
Servant whom everyone would trample on, and become the
militant kind of Messiah so dear to Judas' heart. But Jesus, of
course, would not fulfill Judas' expectations, for they were
another form of the temptations which had persisted
throughout his ministry, and which had been symbolized —
as we saw with Thaddeus-Judas — in Jesus' encounter with
the devil in the desert. In particular, it was the temptation for
Jesus to use his miraculous powers to gain political ends.

According to this answer, it never occurred to Judas that Jesus, even at the cost of his life, would stick with the kind of love which he preached. Rather, Judas expected to precipitate a coup d'etat which would result in Jesus' enthronement in Israel.

Scholars are not agreed, however, that this explanation can be substantiated by the scripture record.

A fourth answer is that avarice was certainly a part of Judas' motivation, or else he would have betrayed Jesus "for free" out of spite. A banking official has stated that 60 percent of the individuals who regularly handle money take money. One evidence of "original sin" is "larceny in the heart." If the bank is right, then only 40 percent of the people who regularly handle money purposefully train themselves in financial integrity! Apparently Judas was numbered among the 60 percent who, in Clarence Buddington Kelland's amusing phrase, "didn't get gifted with honesty."

But what insurrectionist has never been indifferent to money? Jesus was no television evangelist who could bring in thousands of dollars weekly. Judas had only small amounts to handle, which meant that embezzlement was not highly profitable. Perhaps he dreamed, therefore, of becoming Chancellor of the Exchequer in Jesus' new Kingdom, where the pickings would be better. Certainly thirty pieces of silver constituted a modest amount in contrast with Judas' earlier expectations. Yet it was probably more than had been in the disciple's treasury at any one time, so it temporarily satisfied his greed.

Scholars usually accept the fact that avarice was part of Judas' reason for the betrayal.

A final answer suggests the rest of the probable explanation—Judas' personal change of attitude toward Jesus and his Kingdom Crusade. More than being disappointed, eventually Judas become totally disillusioned; and possibly he was also unnerved by fear. There are three references to satanic influences, evil impulses which rose up within him to overpower both his common sense and his moral balance.

We read in Luke: "Then Satan entered into Judas called Iscariot, who was of the number of the twelve; he went away and conferred with the chief priests and captains how he might betray him to them" (Lk.22:3,4 RSV). John adds, "And during supper, when the devil had already put it into the heart of Judas Iscariot, Simon's son, to betray him, Jesus ... rose from the table, laid aside his garments and girded himself with a towel" (Jn.13:2 RSV). "Then, after the morsel, Satan entered into him" (Jn.13:27 RSV).

The basic cause for Judas's allowing the demonic to control his life may be traced to Jesus' patient explanation to his followers that his kingdom was not of this world—neither political, nor military, nor social, but spiritual. He made it plain that he would not raise an army and grind the hated Romans into the dust. Furthermore, he began to prophecy not his own elevation in glory but his forthcoming death.

Two results followed this forthright declaration of Jesus' purposes. One was immediate in its effect. John's Gospel states bluntly, "From that time on, therefore, numbers of his followers deserted him and returned home. Jesus then said to the twelve, 'Will you desert me, too?'

"Simon Peter replied, 'Lord, who else is there to turn to? What you say bears the stamp of the eternal. We know with certainty that you are the Holy One of God'" (Jn.6:66-69). The disciples decided to stick with Jesus—all but one.

For there was also a long-range effect. Then and there Judas may have decided that the Kingdom Crusade was not for him. His former all-out allegiance gradually disintegrated into a sense of having been tricked, and then into a conviction that he had been betrayed by the Master. What is more natural, then, for one who feels betrayed himself, than to get even by betraying his betrayer!

Thus the long-range effect of Jesus' clarification of his mission was to bring Judas at first into concealed but ever-burgeoning hostility toward his Master. Then at some moment not revealed explicitly by Scripture he decided to dissociate himself from a movement doomed to defeat. One suspects that he was also feeling a quickening of personal fear. He had come to realize that he was prominent in a crusade which had been condemned by the authorities, whose leader admitted that his own days were numbered and whose basic purposes he had come to despise. Judas sensed that he would be dragged down in the general ruin unless he repudiated the movement in so dramatic a fashion that everyone would know that he had disavowed his former loyalty. If he could betray his Master to the Establishment, and make a little money on the side, he would save his own skin and be free to find a genuine revolutionary cause to join. So he forced down the angelic powers within him and permitted what was demonic within him to determine his conduct. How human he was, and how contemporary.

The first warning of the betrayal, a warning which the disciples did not heed, is found in the Fourth Gospel. "Jesus said, 'Did I not choose you, the twelve, and one of you is a devil?' He spoke of Judas, the son of Simon Iscariot, for he, one of the twelve, was to betray him" (Jn.6:70,71 RSV).

This was followed by a second warning by Jesus at the last supper, a warning which — undoubtedly to Judas's astonishment — went equally unheeded. Matthew reports that "when it was evening, he sat at the table with the twelve disciples; and as they were eating, he said, 'Truly, I say to you, one of you will betray me'" (Mt.26:20,21 RSV). And when John asked him who it was, "Jesus answered, 'It is he to whom I shall give this morsel when I have dipped it.' So when he had dipped the morsel he gave it to Judas, the son of Simon Iscariot. Then, after the morsel, Satan entered into him. Jesus said to him, 'What you are going to do, do quickly.'

"Now no one at the table knew why he had said this to him. Some thought that, because Judas had the money box, Jesus was telling him, 'Buy what we need for the feast'; or that he should give something to the poor. So, after receiving the morsel, he immediately went out; and it was night." (Jn.13:26-30 RSV).

"And it was night" — one of the most telling sentences in the whole New Testament. It is always night when one betrays another. For he darkens not only his victim's life but also his own. Judas's betrayal not only resulted in Jesus' death, but also his own, after the disintegration of his own character.

Years ago Bonnie Chamberlain wrote in the Saturday Review that hundreds of years ago an artist was commissioned to paint in a Sicilian cathedral a mural depicting the life of Jesus. The painter soon discovered a twelve-year-old lad whose innocent radiance would make a perfect Christ-Child, and used him as a model. Over the years the mural developed till it reached the events of Holy Week. One by one the key figures were completed till only the person of Judas remained undone.

One afternoon a man whose face was seamed with dissipation lurched into the tavern where the artist was sitting. At once the painter saw that here was his terribly perfect model for the remaining figure. He led the man to the cathedral and pointing to the bare space on the wall, asked him to pose for Judas.

To his astonishment the wino burst out crying and hid his face in his hands. "Don't you remember me, Maestro?" Pointing to the Christ-Child, he added, "Years ago I was your model for him!"

Is this not also the tragedy of Judas himself? Hester Cholmondeley describes it in this manner:

> "Still as of old
>   Man by himself is priced:
> For thirty pieces Judas sold
>   Himself, not Christ!

This is true in every generation. A farmer drove his grain truck on to the elevator scales and walked quietly around to the far side to step surreptitiously on the scales. The operator noted the total weight on the sales credit slip and handed the carbon copy to the farmer.

"Well, Joe," he said, "You just sold yourself for about twelve dollars."

For that farmer, suddenly it was night!

C. His Remorse

When Judas had seen Jesus manacled and the eleven disciples flee for their lives, he quietly left the Garden. He had done what he had contracted for. No record indicates that he stayed around for the trial, but he must have followed closely the events. There are only three more references to him, and two deal with the manner of his dying. The First Gospel shows him so remorseful that he commits suicide: Acts makes him still acquisitive and the victim of an unexplained accident.

But first, the remorse, "When Judas, who had betrayed him, learned that Jesus had been condemned to death, he was filled with remorse. Taking the thirty pieces of silver back to the chief priests and elders, he cried, 'I have done a great wrong, for I have caused the death of an innocent man.'

"'What do we care?' they answered. 'That is your worry!'

"Judas threw the silver on to the temple floor and went out and hanged himself."

In his "Ammergau," F. W. H. Meyers makes this comment:

When in his rage he could no longer bear
Men's voices nor the sunlight nor the air,
Nor sleep, nor waking, nor his own quick breath,
Nor God in heaven, nor anything but death —
I bowed my head, and through my fingers ran
Tears for the end of that Iscariot man,
Lost, in the hopeless struggle of the soul
To make the done undone, the broken whole.

"Picking up the money, the chief priests said, 'This is blood money. It would not be right to put it into the treasury.' So after discussion they used it to buy a potter's field, to serve as a cemetery for foreigners. And to this very day that place is knowns as the 'Field of Blood'" (Mt.27:3-8).

The record in Acts is as follows: "Now this man bought a field with the reward of his wickedness; and falling headlong he burst open in the middle and all his bowels gushed out. And it became known to all the inhabitants of Jerusalem, so that the field was called, in their language, Akeldama, that is, Field of Blood" (Ac.1:18,19 RSV).

History and human nature have inclined toward Matthew's version. This may be due partly to the fact that the account in Acts seems to be based on a similar event in the Story of Ahiqar, and partly because Matthew's assumes the basic Christian belief that every soul is reformable even though it has betrayed what is holiest. But the Christian Church has not always accepted this belief.

During his ordination examination a seminary classmate of mine was being asked a series of doctrinal questions by an elderly minister. He came to this question: "Do you believe in the Doctrine of the Total Depravity of the Human Soul?"

The candidate brought down the house with his immediate smiling reply. "Yes, but I find it very difficlut to live up to!"

The candidate may have misunderstood the doctrine, but his answer was most suitable! Judas tried hard to live up to it. He failed, however, because, God's redemptive power being absolute, he was not beyond redemption. His failure to be "totally depraved" showed in his remorse, which is the first step in salvation — acknowledging that wrong has been done and expressing sorrow and shame. A second step is to make such restitution as is possible. A third step is to ask forgiveness of the one wronged; and a fourth step is to accept such forgiveness gratefully and make a fresh start.

A friend once described the traumatic experience of stealing a packet of Life Savers from his mother's pocketbook. He took them out behind the barn and settled down to enjoy them. "The first tasted absolutely delicious," he said. "The second, unaccountably, was a bit bitter. And with the third, I was through eating. A growing uneasiness and remorse had begun to turn my taste buds sour. I knew that I had sinned my way out of my mother's trust. In shame I took the packet back into the house and confessed my theft to her. Forgiveness bright as a summer cloud engulfed me, and I was restored to the wholesomeness I once knew."

Remorse, restitution, forgiveness, restoration! The third and fourth were denied Judas. He felt remorse and tried to make restitution of the blood money. How genuine that remorse was is indicated by the fact that he left the silver in the temple — an uncharacteristic gesture. But he could not ask forgiveness of Jesus who was under death-row guard, and therefore could not have a sense of being restored to the divine love. Lacking these essential steps, he thereby felt himself damned. So he took the only course his despair could offer, that of suicide.

But he did not realize that "God has no pleasure in the death of the wicked, but that the wicked turn from his way and live" (Ez.33:11 RSV). Suicide was not the only course of action open to him. He might have confessed his sin and shame to the disciples and to God, and declared that his whole life would be spent in making restitution as he was able. If the disciples had believed this — and there are grounds for doubting that they would have then — they would have taken him back on probation till he had proved the integrity of his declarations. But if they had not, he could have depended on God. A redeemed, devoted Judas would have contributed greatly to the strength of the young churches.

One has only to look at another man who was Judas'

contemporary, named Paul. He hated Christians so much that he rejoiced when Jesus died, watched approvingly when a mob stoned Stephen the Martyr, and was the fiercest enemy of the young churches. There is no record of the number of Christian deaths for which he may have been responsible. Then the Lord stopped him cold on the Damascus Road and filled him with a keen sense of wrongdoing. As he thought in despair of the havoc he had worked among the Christians, he must have considered that suicide might be the best way out of a hopeless situation. But Ananias showed him forgiveness, brought him into the church fellowship and set his feet on the path which led to saintliness. It would be impossible to calculate what the world would be like today had Paul yielded to the temptation to take his own life!

In like manner, would Judas not finally have realized the full potential which Jesus saw in him when calling him, had he elected to live and turn his remorse into driving energy for his Lord? This might have happened had he not been so precipitate. He did not even wait to see whether Jesus actually would be put to death. Had he delayed, and then learned of the resurrection, how differently would he have reacted? Would the future have seemed to be so unbearable after all? We do not know.

But one thing is certain: had he waited, he would have had Jesus' forgiveness and restoration of the forfeited relationship. There are legends enshrining this conviction. Robert Buchanan has set one into verse, describing how Judas' soul, condemned to seeking the dark places, comes on a cottage blazing with light. Through the window he can see a table set as if for Holy Communion. He pauses, realizing that he had left the original Upper Room before Jesus instituted the Last Supper. But he sees Jesus standing in the doorway, beckoning him to enter. As he fearfully creeps near, the Master says to him gently,

"The holy Supper is spread within,
And many candles shine;
And I have waited long for thee
Before I poured the wine."

And for the first time, Judas received Communion.

In his memoirs, *The Days of Our Years*, Pierre van Paassen records a conversation he had with a Dutch priest who had survived the terrors of Nazi occupation but who spoke of the Germans in forgiveness.

"'You are too kind, M. l'Abbé,' I said. 'You already seem to have forgotten how they behaved. You have an excuse for everybody. You would have a good word even for a damned soul like Judas.'

"'A damned soul? Judas?' The Abbé suddenly placed his hand on my arm. 'Why do you say that, my son?' I turned around. The flame from the candle lit up his fine face. He brushed a strand of silver hair from his forehead. I knew that he was deeply perturbed.

"'You should not say that, my son,' he said, and I noticed that his voice trembled with emotion. 'Let us not be hasty in our judgments. You must not say of any man that he is a lost soul. We are not the judge of that. For you may depend on it,' he went on earnestly, 'that if Judas in that terrible moment when he hanged himself and just before he lost consciousness entirely, if in that moment, I say, he sighed his regret and his repentance, I assure you, my son, that that sigh was heard in heaven and that the first drop of Jesus' blood was shed for Judas Iscariot.'"

If Jesus, the victim, would forgive Judas, why should not Jesus' disciples in every generation forgive him?

And if Judas could receive forgiveness, who cannot?

Chapter Eight

The Thirteenth Disciple

IF the disciples has been worried about appointing a thirteenth disciple who would receive all the superstition which gathers around that number, the death of Judas ended that worry. Judas, the twelfth, had taken on himself all the ill-luck and evil attributable to the thirteenth, leaving that spot free of any onus. Besides, with Judas gone, the disciples, with a replacement, would still only number twelve. So as the church began to rally to its mission, Acts relates, "Peter stood up among the brethren (the company of persons was in all about a hundred and twenty), and said, 'Brethren, the Scripture had to be fulfilled, which the Holy Spirit spoke beforehand by the mouth of David, concerning Judas who was guide to those who arrested Jesus. For he was numbered among us, and was allotted his share in this ministry.... For it is written in the Book of Psalms, "Let his habitation become desolate, and let there be no one to live in it," and "His office let another take."

"'So one of the men who have accompanied us all during the time that the Lord Jesus went in and out among us, beginning from the baptism of John until the day he was taken up from us —one of these men must become with us a witness to his resurrection.'

"And they put forward two, Joseph called Barsabbas, who was surnamed Justus, and Matthias. And they prayed and said, 'Lord, thou who knowest the hearts of all men, show which one of these two thou hast chosen to take the place in this ministry and apostleship from which Judas turned aside, to go to his own place.' And they cast lots for them, and the lot fell on Matthias, and he was enrolled with the eleven apostles" (Ac.1:15-17,20-26 RSV).

Who was Matthias? We do not know. If one visualizes the followers of Jesus extending outward from their central Master in concentric rings, then Peter, James and John constituted the innermost ring; the next included the other nine disciples; the third ring contained followers of longest and most dedicated participation; and so on out to the final ring of the curious and the halfhearted. Undoubtedly both candidates for the vacancy held seniority in the third ring, which contained about six dozen persons. But what part Matthias played in advancing the worldwide cause of the Kingdom Crusade is not known. He is said to have written a book entitled, "The Traditions of Matthias," which is now lost; but whoever wrote it in his name lived a century later than he. The only tradition which may be true is the claim of the Armenian Church that Matthias was one of its founders.

In New York's Riverside Church many saints occupy niches throughout the gothic structure. But there are also empty niches awaiting the saints whom the future will produce. Now in a sense Matthias' niche is empty because there are no facts with which to clothe the name with flesh and personality. This then makes it possible for me to offer as a thirteenth disciple someone I know very well indeed —myself. For you the thirteenth disciple could be yourself. This would not be an act of pride or self-aggrandizement but of devotion and dedication. In these times there is no excuse for bashfulness on your part or mine to add our names to the roster of the disciples. Neither of us is perfect, of course, but neither were they, at first. We are closed-minded, and that is the way the Twelve began. We are self-centered, and this was true of them all. We are familiar with self-distrust, skepticism and fear, and so were the disciples. If they grew into Christian maturity, so can we! It is thoughtless to exclaim, "But look! they had the presence of their Master to hearten them!" for do not we as well? Thus every follower needs to respond to the call, "Who is on the Lord's side?" by standing up boldly to be counted. We ourselves not only need to work at such a stirring challenge, but the society in which we live must also see firsthand through us what the Christian Way, the Truth and the Life are all about. Is this not the primary function of every thirteenth disciple?

For consider this — that individuals about us have for years been examining the day-by-day record of our lives. Our neighbors and friends are aware that we confess the Christian faith. Each Monday, then, they may be reading us afresh, without our realizing it, to see if we made any spiritual discoveries the day before which will make a difference the day after. If there are few observable changes in us over the months, they are apt to conclude one of three things:

1. that Christianity is greatly over-rated and that they are justified in having nothing to do with it;
2. that the church is running largely on ancient reputation, and that they do well to stay away from it; or
3. that Christianity and the church are all right, but that *we* are impervious to their influence!

But on the other hand, when from month to month they can see that we are being changed, however minutely, by contact with God through the living Christ and through the fellowship of his present-day followers, they may say to themselves, "Hmm! Look what's happening to that fellow! (Or to that woman, or youth, or even to that old goat!) Maybe there's something to Christianity, after all!"

To live in faith during these tumultuous times is the responsibility of a thirteenth disciple.

And it is an inescapable duty. Years ago Thomas Chalmers wrote: "Every man is a missionary now and forever, for good or evil, whether he intends it or not. He may be a blot, radiating his dark influence outward to the very circumference of society; or he may be a blessing, spreading benediction over the length and breadth of the world; but a blank he cannot be." The twelfth disciple, Judas, chose the dark; it is the opportunity of a thirteenth disciple to choose the light, heeding the words which Paul wrote to the new Christians in the pagan city of Philippi: "Let the lives you lead be worthy of the Good News of Christ" (1:27). If the Christian faith is to have a determining impact on life today, it will be only because Jesus' contemporary disciples learn the prayer which Frank Laubach taught the savage Moros: "Lord, put a light behind my eyes that will shine out, so that people can see Jesus through me."

Philotheos Zikas relates that during his evangelizing years in Muslim-dominated Thrace, a villager once said to him, "We have read the Christian Bible, we have enjoyed the Gospels, we recognize Jesus as the world's greatest man. But it puzzles us that the Christians in our village don't really live any differently from us. It makes us feel that there is no good reason for us to leave Islam to become Christian. If these Christians would live the beliefs of the Bible, more of us would become Christian."

Exactly! The time is now, the need immediate. Dr. J. H. Cockburn, has stated unequivocally, "The anti-Christian forces of Communism and Fascism cannot be argued down or shot down; they must be lived down. Christianity has truth on its side. But that truth must be demonstrated in living terms if Christian civilization is to survive." The thirteenth disciple must incarnate the faith.

Baroness Isak Dinesen, who lived for years on a lovely farm in the highlands of Nairobi, wrote a classic entitled, *Out of Africa*. She told about a young Kikuyu named Kitau who became her houseboy. "After three months," she wrote "he asked me one day to give him a letter of recommendation to my old friend Sheik Ali Ben Salim. I did not want Kitau to leave just when he had learned the routine of the house, and I said that I would raise his pay. No, he said, he was not leaving to get any higher pay, but that he had made up his mind that he would either become a Christian or a Mohammedan, only he did not know which yet. For this reason he had come and worked with me for three months in my house to see the ways and the habits of the Christians. From me he would go for three months to Sheik Ali in Mombassa, and study the ways and habits of the Mohammedans. Then he would decide.

"My heavens!" the Baroness exclaimed, as remembrances of her obvious imperfections in dealing with him came rushing into mind. "Why didn't you tell me."

Would she not have been less troubled and embarrassed if throughout those crucial ninety days she had consciously been serving the Lord as a thirteenth disciple?

The Director of the Columbia Recording Company of London has related that his firm once contracted with Albert Schweitzer to make twelve Bach organ recordings. "Dr. Schweitzer arrived in Southampton one Saturday morning," he wrote, "and we set about to find a church whose organ he would play on. We also had to find the right sort of person to go with him to arrange for setting up the microphones and all that. Finally, after going through our staff carefully, we selected a young man we felt sure he would like.

"Off they went together the next day, and it took several weeks to finish the series. But let me tell you about that young man himself. Nothing had been said about his being a person of religious devotion. All that we had sought was a smart young man who would know just what Dr. Schweitzer needed. All through the days they worked together, nothing was said about religion—we learned that from the young man himself. But when he came back to our head office, he was a transformed individual!" He had been in the company of a thirteenth disciple.

One of the great audacities of history occurred when twelve men set themselves against the increasingly degenerate and disintegrating society in which they lived—the Roman Empire which had conquered three-quarters of the known world. These men began a process of "catching people" for God, which finally lifted that Empire off its hinges as Samson lifted the gates of Gaza and sent it off to history's scrap heap.

A favorite indoor sport today is to compare American society with that of Rome in the year 400 and lay bets as to whether for America there are more than the 76 years which remained for Rome. It is a gruesome game because there are an alarming number of parallels.

But the fact that history tends to repeat itself is not necessarily doom-producing. America will not "fall" just because Rome "fell"—unless we refuse to learn from the past and allow similar seeds of destruction to flourish unchecked within us. If we permit the same moral and spiritual collapse which happened to the Roman Empire to occur within our own nation, then of course the American Republic is doomed indeed.

But history's ability to repeat itself also offers a positive hope. For small groups of Jesus' present-day thirteenth disciples, under the impulse of the Holy Spirit in a new Pentecost, once again can repeat the earlier miracle and bring saving life into a disordered and disoriented American society.

The immediate question is this: will there be enough of such disciples to re-enact the miracle of the Early Church?

> The twelve disciples long are dead,
>   And faithful Saint Matthias, too;
> The souls of Paul and Mark are sped —
>   So Christ must turn to me and you.
>
> His haunting voice now calls again
>   As once it spoke in Galilee;
> "I need your help in catching men,
>   So come at once and follow me!"

INDEX

INDEX